Bread of Life Christian Fellowship's
Foundations of Faith

Copyright owned by
Betty Sue Tracy.
2009
All rights reserved

Christian Living
P.O. Box 20009
Carson City, Nevada, 89721
Breadoflifecf.com.com
978-0-9779951-7-2

The right of reproduction of this book is reserved exclusively for the author who grants permission for brief quotes to be used for review purposes as long as full credit is given to the author.
Copies may be made for use within your own family. For use within a church or study group please contact the above address.

"Thou shalt not muzzle the ox that treadeth out the corn. And, the laborer is worthy of his reward." 1 Timothy 5:18 (1 Corinthians 9:9, Deuteronomy 25:4, Luke 10:7, Matthew 10:10, Deuteronomy 24:15.)
"Therefore, behold, I am against the prophets, saith the Lord, that steal my words every one from his neighbor." Jeremiah 23:30
:...Thou shalt not steal, ... Thou shalt love thy neighbor as thyself." Romans 13:9 (Matthew 19:18, Mark 10:19, Luke 18:20, 1 Corinthians 6:8,10, Ephesians 4:28, Exodus 20:15, Leviticus 19:11,13, Deuteronomy 5:19, Leviticus 19:18, Matthew 5,:43, 7:12, 19:19, 22,:39, Mark 12:31, Luke 10:27, Galatians 5:14, James 2:8)
"Render therefore to all their dues: ... honor to whom honor." Romans 13:7
"That no man go beyond and defraud his brother in any matter: because that the Lord is the avenger of all such, as we also have forewarned you and testified." 1 Thessalonians 4:6 (Leviticus 19:13, Deuteronomy 32:35, Proverbs 22:22,23)
Scriptures compiled by the Bluedorns, Triviumpursuit.com.

Cover picture by James Tracy.

1. Can I Believe the Bible? 4
2. Is There A God? 6
3. Jesus Christ of Nazareth 9
4. What Is The Character Of God? 12
5. Why Must I Get Saved? 20
6. Assurance of Salvation 26
7. How Do I Discover God's Will? 33
8. How to Overcome Temptation 36
9. Learning To Pray 41
10. How to Read the Bible 52
11. Facts About The Bible 58
12. Which Bible to Use 63
13. Bible Helps 66
14. Church Attendance 71
15. Water Baptism 78
16. The Gift of the Holy Ghost 80
17. Home Worship, Family Alter and Quiet Time 85
18. Witnessing 92
19. Tithing and Stewardship 94
20. Our church 99

1. Can I Believe the Bible?

The Bible was written by eyewitnesses to the events they record. This is the gold standard for historical evidence. If the person that experienced the event writes it, it is accepted as truth.

No other document in the history of the world has been as thoroughly challenged, examined, torn apart, and criticized. Yet, the Bible has NEVER been proven wrong.

There have been times when people claimed to have proven it wrong. It was said, "King David never existed. He was just a legend". Within two years of this statement, archeologists dug up his signet ring; positive proof he did exist. They have said the same thing about Nineveh, Babylon, and the Hittites. Same results. It almost looks like God is withholding the physical evidence until someone says something in the Bible doesn't exist and then He allows the remains to be discovered to make the scientists look like fools. Who says God doesn't have a sense of humor?

The fact is that, whether they like it or not, science is continually proving more and more of the Bible to be right. For example, 3000 years ago King Solomon said,

> Proverbs 16:24 "**Pleasant __ __ __ __ __ are as an honeycomb, sweet to the soul, and health to the bones.**"

How did Solomon know honey was good for the bones? This is something science just discovered in the last century.

If I can't believe the Bible, then I can't believe any other ancient document. None of them can stand up to the same standards of examination until about 1100AD. If the Bible isn't true, then Buddha, Confucius, Caesar, Hannibal, Justinian, Nero, Plato, Aristotle, Socrates and many, many others never existed. There is no proof of their existence that even comes close to being as scientifically and historically reliable as the Bible.

There are many prophecies in the Bible that have been fulfilled. Only Someone who knew the beginning from the end could have told Isaiah that a man named Cyrus would send the Israelites back to their homeland…seventy years before Cyrus was born!

> Isaiah 44:8 **"That said of Cyrus, He is my __ __ __ __ __ __ __ __, and shall perform all my pleasure: even saying to Jerusalem, You shall be built; and to the temple, Your foundation shall be laid."**

Jeremiah prophesied that Judah would be in captivity for seventy years, and they were.

Abraham received word that his descendants would leave Egypt in 400 years and they did.

Joseph received interpretation of dreams that came true.

Daniel received and recorded several prophecies about the rise and fall of Babylon, Medo-Persia, Greece, Syria, and Rome in extreme detail, plus an exact time table for the time of the Messiah. All of this came true exactly as predicted.

The prophecies concerning Christ Himself are mathematically impossible for one man to fulfill (He shall come from Nazareth, come up from Egypt, AND come from Bethlehem, for example) and yet Christ fulfilled EVERY ONE!

If the Bible is true historically and scientifically and its prophecies have proven true in the face of astronomical odds, there is no logical reason to doubt it spiritually.

I can believe.

2. Is There A God?

This is the fundamental question of life on which all other questions hang. If there is no God then life has no purpose beyond my momentary pleasure. There is no meaning. There is no right or wrong. I should take all I can get and enjoy myself for the moment because when it is over, it is OVER. "That's all she wrote," so to speak.

If there is a God, however, then there is a heaven to gain and a hell to shun; a Great White Throne to stand in front of and give answer to. There is a right and a wrong. There is an eternity that is more real than anything I have every experienced in my life, good or bad.

Can I know if there is a God? And if so, how?

The human soul demands a God. Even Atheists know this in their hearts. That is why they get so upset at the mention of God. They don't get mad at the mention of Santa Claus, the Easter Bunny, the Tooth fairy, Buddha, Mohammed, or any other religious or fictional character. Only the Christian God angers them. This tells me that in their heart, they know He is true.

The atheist's very assertion that if there was a God, He wouldn't allow evil in the world acknowledges that they know good and evil in their hearts, a sign of the design of God Himself. They, themselves, wouldn't even know there is evil in the world if God hadn't written "right and wrong" on the human heart.

Within the cells of every living organism is a thing called DNA. This is the programming that determines whether I am a watermelon or a human, whether I have blue eyes or brown, whether I am tall or short. This DNA is an intricate code that we humans are just now beginning to be able to read.

Noah Webster says:
CODE,
n. Any collection or digest of laws.

LAW,
n. [L. lex; A law is that which is laid, set or fixed, like statute, constitution, from L. statuo.]

2. Is There a God?

1. A rule, particularly an established or permanent rule, prescribed by the supreme power of a state to its subjects, for regulating their actions, particularly their social actions. Laws are imperative or mandatory, commanding what shall be done; prohibitory, restraining from what is to be forborne; or permissive, declaring what may be done without incurring a penalty. The laws which enjoin the duties of piety and morality are prescribed by God and found in the Scriptures.

I do not have green vines coming out of my ears, grapes hanging off my nose, or a horse-like tail because the laws prescribed by the Supreme Power who wrote my DNA says I don't.

Could my DNA have written itself?
No. DNA is a language. Language takes intelligence.

LAN'GUAGE, n. [L. lingua, the tongue, and speech.]
Words duly arranged in sentences, written, printed or engraved, and exhibited to the eye. (DNA is exhibited to the eye through the microscope. Different from my glasses only in degree) *Style; manner of expression. Any manner of expressing thoughts.*

"Any manner of expressing thoughts." For DNA to express thoughts there had to be thoughts to express before it was written down in my cells. There has to be a Creator God.

I will look at the giraffe.

Their necks are so tall they must have an extraordinarily strong heart in order to pump the blood all the way up there. But with such a strong heart, if they bend their head down, gravity + the heart would blow their brains out (high blood pressure). So they have a set of valves in the arteries of their necks that shut the blood flow down when they put their head down. But then when they lift their heads suddenly (as in a lion attack) they would pass out (low blood pressure). So they have little sponges in the back of their brains that hold enough blood in reserve to keep them conscious until the valves open again. If any one of these steps was missing, the giraffe would die (either by exploding brain or hungry lion). They must have all been there from the start. They could not have evolved. They must have been created as a complete animal.

2. Is There a God?

There are many other creatures (the woodpecker who would knock its eyes out if it had not been programmed to close its eyes with each strike, the garden spider which would starve if its web was not just right, the chicken egg where the chick would suffocate without its microscopic air holes, the human eye, the bombardier beetle which would blow itself up if it did not have all systems functioning at once, etc.) that simply could not exist without a Divine Design .

There must be a God.

3.   Jesus Christ of Nazareth

Let us look at Jesus.

It is a historical fact that Jesus of Nazareth existed, preached, and was executed by the Romans at the insistence of the Jewish leaders. Secular history says this much. No other historical figure has as much evidence for his existence.

All Jesus would have had to do to avoid being executed in the most torturous way humans have ever come up with was to say He was not God. That is all. Yet He went to the cross with the words "I am (God)" on His lips.

➢ Mark 14:61 **"Again the high priest asked him, and said unto him, "Art thou the __ __ __ __ __ __, the Son of the Blessed?" And Jesus said, "__ __ __: and ye shall see the Son of man sitting on the right hand of power, and coming in the clouds of heaven."**

Why would He do this?

There are only two possibilities. He either was God or He was not.

There is no in between.

I am either God or I am not (I will tell you right now that I am not). The chair I am sitting in is either God or it is not. There is no in between.

If Jesus was not God, He either knew He was not or He did not know He was not. Again, there is no in-between.

Jesus was either a liar, a lunatic or He really was Lord.

Liars, con-artists, are capable of convincing large numbers of people that they are divine. But they all have one thing in common: a strong sense of Self Preservation. A liar of the magnitude Christ would have had to be to pull off the things He did, would have been able to work out a deal with the Jews to avoid being crucified. The fact that He didn't even try shows that the man actually believed what He was saying. Anyone who honestly believes He is God (enough to go to the Cross for that belief) is either coo-coo or God Himself. No alternatives.

3. Jesus Christ of Nazareth

The level of insanity that convinces a man He is God (strongly enough to override the self-preservation instinct) is called Complex, Paranoid Schizophrenia. We have many examples of this disease available for study. Charles Manson is probably the most famous modern case. All victims of Complex, Paranoid Schizophrenia have one thing in common; they are very violent. Charles Manson committed his crimes (slaughtering a houseful of people) trying to start a race war that would allow him to take over the world.

- He who lives by the sword shall die by the sword.
- Love your neighbor as yourself.
- Do good to them that wrongfully use you.
- Turn the other cheek.

These are quotes from Christ. Do these sound like the rantings of a violent lunatic? What about the results of His teaching?

➢ Matthew 7:16 **"You shall know them by their __ __ __ __ __ __ ."**

Christianity has been the greatest force for peace and brotherly love in history all over the world. Christianity is responsible for the elimination of cannibalism, stopping countless feuds and wars, stopping human sacrifice. It is also known that the more non-Catholic missionaries an African country had in the last two centuries, the more educated and equal their women are and the freer their people are in general. Is this the fruit of Complex, Paranoid Schizophrenia? I don't think so.

"Once you have eliminated all the possibilities, what ever remains, no matter how implausible, must be the truth."
(Sherlock Holmes)

If Christ was not a liar; if He was not a lunatic; He must be Lord.

"There is a God, and you are not Him."
Andrew Tracy

The Romans who crucified Christ were experts at execution. Those soldiers would have lost their heads if they did not do it right, so they always made sure they did. Christ was dead when He was removed from the cross.

They placed Him in a tomb and rolled a stone so heavy that three healthy women (who were used to the normal hard labor of the pre-electronic age) were concerned they would not be able to move it away enough to get in. They sealed the tomb with wax and placed guards around it that, again, would lose their heads if they did not do their job right. Christ was not in a coma, as some have claimed. There is no way He could have moved that boulder to get out, even if He had been perfectly healthy, and especially not just three days after the ordeal of the cross (with no water, food or medicine in the meantime).

The disciples did not steal the body. The soldiers (somewhere between 12 and 20 of them) would have killed them if they had tried (and these are the same men who had just run away when Jesus was arrested. Hardly the examples of courage necessary to attack trained soldiers.)

Every disciple but John was later executed for claiming Christ was alive. Again, these men's teachings were those of sane men ("Love your neighbor as yourself"), yet they died for the belief that Christ rose from the dead. They obviously believed it.

In addition, they had just spent three and a half years living day and night with Christ. They could not have been fooled about His identity. When they said they saw their Lord AFTER His crucifixion, all reasonable evidence says that is exactly what they saw; the risen Jesus Christ.

4. What Is The Character Of God?

Who is God?

God has chosen to reveal Himself to me in the Bible. Only by reading It can I come to know Him. Some of the names of God in the Bible are:

Advocate,
Almighty,
Ancient of Days,
Author and Finisher,
Baptizer,
Bishop and Guardian of Our Souls,
Chief Apostle,
Chief Cornerstone,
Christ (Messiah),
Comforter,
Counselor,
Daystar,
Deliverer,
Everlasting Father,
Everlasting God,
First Born,
God of Everlasting Time,
God of Seeing,
God of the Covenant,
God Our Righteousness,
God Our Rock,
Godhead,
Great High Priest,
Head of the Body,
Highest,
Holy One,
Immanuel (God Is With Us),
Jealous (he wants nothing between him and us),
Judge,
King of Kings,
Father,
Lamb of God,
Lamb Slain Before the Foundation of the World,
Last (Or Second) Adam,
Lord (Boss),
Lord God Almighty,
Lord God,
Lord of Lords,
Master,
Mighty God,
Mighty One,
Our Banner,
Our Peace,
Physician,
Pioneer and Perfecter of Our Faith,
Potentate,
Prince of Peace,
Redeemer,
Righteous One,
Rock,
Root of Jesse,
Salvation (Jesus),
Sanctifier,
Savior,
Seven Fold Spirit,
Shepherd,
Shield,
Spirit of God,
Spirit of Grace,
Spirit of Holiness,
Spirit of Life,
Spirit of Mercy,
Spirit of Truth,
Stone,
Strength,
Strengthener,
The Anointed One,
The Branch,
The First and the Last,
The I Am,
The Lord Is There,
The Lord of Hosts,
The Most High,
The One Who Heals,
The One Who Sanctifies,
The Sun of Righteousness,
Wonderful,

4. What is the Character of God?

But What IS God?
God is the eternal, creative Spirit. He made everything, knows everything, and is everywhere at the same time.

- John 4:24 **"God is a __ __ __ __ __ __: and they that worship Him must worship Him in __ __ __ __ __ __ and in __ __ __ __ __."**

- Genesis 1:1 **"In the beginning, God __ __ __ __ __ __ __ the __ __ __ __ __ __ __ and the __ __ __ __ __."**

- Genesis 21:33 **"And Abraham planted a grove in Beersheba, and called there on the name of the Lord, the __ __ __ __ __ __ __ __ __ __ God."**

- Deuteronomy 33:27 **"The __ __ __ __ __ __ __ God is thy refuge, and underneath are the __ __ __ __ __ __ __ __ __ __ __ arms: and he shall thrust out the enemy from before thee; and shall say, Destroy them."**

- Job 37:16 **"Dost thou know the balancings of the clouds, the wondrous works of Him which is perfect in __ __ __ __ __ __ __ __ __?"**

- Psalms 90:2 **"Before the __ __ __ __ __ __ __ __ __ were brought forth, or ever Thou hadst formed the __ __ __ __ __ and the world, even from __ __ __ __ __ __ __ __ __ to everlasting, Thou art God."**

- Psalms 139:2-16 **"Thou knowest my __ __ __ __ __ __ __ __ __ __ and mine __ __ __ __ __ __ __ __; Thou understandest my thought afar off…**

    v4 For there is not a word in my __ __ __ __ __ __, but, lo, O Lord, Thou knowest it altogether…

    v7 Whither shall I go from Thy __ __ __ __ __ __? Or wither shall I flee from Thy __ __ __ __ __ __ __ __?

    v8 If I ascend up into __ __ __ __ __ __, Thou art there: if I make my bed in __ __ __ __, behold, Thou art there.

4. What is the Character of God?

v9 If I take the wings of the morning, and _____ in the uttermost parts of the ___;

v10 Even _____ shall Thy hand lead me, and Thy right hand shall hold me.

v11 If I say, 'Surely the _____ shall cover me; even the night shall be light about me.'

v12 Yea, the darkness hideth not from ____; but the night shineth as the ___: the darkness and the light are both _____ to Thee…

v14 I will praise Thee; for I am _____ and _____ made: marvelous are Thy works; and that my soul knoweth right well.

v15 My substance was not hid from Thee when I was made in the _____, and curiously wrought in the lowest parts of the earth.

v16 Thine eyes did see my _____, yet being unperfect; and in Thy book all my members were written which in continuance were fashioned, when as yet there was none of them."

What is God's character?

- 1 John 4:8 "He that loveth not knoweth not God; for God is _____."

- 1 John 4:16 "And we have known and _____ the love that God hath to us. God is love; and he that dwelleth in ____ dwelleth in God, and God in him."

- 1 John 4:10 "Herein is ____, not that we loved God, but that He loved us, and sent His ___ to be the propitiation (payment) for our ____."

God is Love.

4. What is the Character of God?

- Job 37:23 "Touching the Almighty, we cannot find Him out: He is excellent in power, and in __ __ __ __ __ __ __, and in plenty of __ __ __ __ __ __ __: He will not afflict."

    If God wanted to harm me, He could. He does not need to wait for my acknowledgment of Him or for my permission. However, He chooses to love me instead.

- Psalms 89:14 "Justice and judgment are the habitation of Thy throne: __ __ __ __ __ and __ __ __ __ __ shall go before Thy face."

- Isaiah 9:7 "Of the increase of His __ __ __ __ __ __ __ __ __ and peace there shall be no end, upon the throne of David, and upon His __ __ __ __ __ __, to order it, and to establish it with judgment and with __ __ __ __ __ __ __ from henceforth even forever. The zeal of the LORD of hosts will perform this."

- Jeremiah 23:5 "Behold, the days come, saith the LORD, that I will raise unto David a righteous __ __ __ __ __ __, and a King shall reign and prosper, and shall execute __ __ __ __ __ __ __ and justice in the earth."

    God is Justice.

- Philippians 4:19 "But my God shall supply all your __ __ __ __ according to His riches in glory by Christ Jesus."

- Psalms 23:1 "The LORD is my __ __ __ __ __ __ __ __; I shall not want (have needs)."

- Psalms 34:9 "O fear the LORD, ye His saints: for there is no want (needs) to them that __ __ __ __ Him."

- Psalms 34:10 "The young lions do lack, and suffer hunger: but they that __ __ __ __ the LORD shall not want (be lacking) any __ __ __ __ thing."

- Proverbs 13:25 "The righteous eateth to the __ __ __ __ __ __ __ __ __ of his soul: but the belly of the wicked shall want (be empty)."

> Philippians 4:11 "**Not that I speak in respect of want** (need): **for I have learned, in whatsoever state I am, therewith to be _ _ _ _ _ _ _."**

God is my Supplier.

If God is love and He is the supplier of all my needs and He is just, then if He tells me to do something, He will give me all I need to do it. He will not tell me to do something and then sit back and laugh at me while I flounder. I can depend on His supplying all I need. I can't always tell where that supply will come from and God often waits until what seems to me to be the last minute to give me those supplies in order to build my faith that HE will supply. But I CAN depend on Him. So the next natural question is…

What Does God Want From Me? What Is My Purpose In Life?

This is an important question to ask.

> Ecclesiastics 12:13 "**Let us hear the conclusion of the whole matter: _ _ _ _ God, and keep His _ _ _ _ _ _ _ _ _ _ _: for this is the whole duty of man** (kind)."

> John 14:15 "**If ye _ _ _ _ Me, keep My commandments.**"

> Matthew 19:17 "**And He said unto him, 'Why callest thou Me good? There is none good but one, that is, God: but if thou wilt _ _ _ _ _ into _ _ _ _, keep the commandments.'**"

> John 15:10 "**If ye keep My commandments, ye shall _ _ _ _ _ in My_ _ _ _; even as I have kept My Father's _ _ _ _ _ _ _ _ _ _ _, and abide in His love.**"

> 1John 2:3 "**And _ _ _ _ _ _ we do know that we know Him; if we _ _ _ _ His commandments.**"

> 1 John 5:2 "**By this we know that we _ _ _ _ the children of God, when we love God, and _ _ _ _ His commandments.**"

4. What is the Character of God?

OK, He wants me to keep His commandments. What are they?

➢ Deuteronomy 6:1,5 **"Now these are the
__ __ __ __ __ __ __ __ __ __ __, the statutes, and the
judgments, which the LORD your God commanded to
__ __ __ __ __ you, …**

    v4 **Hear, O Israel: The __ __ __ __ our God is one __ __ __ __:
And thou shalt __ __ __ __ the LORD thy God with all thin
__ __ __ __ __, and with all thy __ __ __ __, and with all thy
__ __ __ __ __."**

➢ Matthew 22:37-40 **"Jesus said unto him, 'Thou shalt love the
__ __ __ __ thy God with __ __ __ thy heart, and with __ __ __ thy
soul, and with __ __ __ thy mind. This is the __ __ __ __ __ and
great commandment. And the __ __ __ __ __ __ is like unto it, Thou
shalt love thy __ __ __ __ __ __ __ __ as thyself. On these two
commandments hang all the __ __ __ and the
__ __ __ __ __ __ __ __.'"**

So if I Love God more than anything else in the world and love my neighbors as much as I love myself I am obeying all the laws and commandments contained in the Bible.

I am to love God more than anything or anyone else in the world. He is to not only be my first priority, but interwoven into all my other priorities.

I might ask with the lawyer speaking to Jesus;
➢ Luke 10:29b **"And who is my __ __ __ __ __ __ __ __?"**

Jesus responds by telling him the story we now call "The Good Samaritan."

➢ Luke 10:30-36 **"And Jesus answering said, 'A certain man went down from Jerusalem to Jericho, and fell among thieves, which stripped him of his raiment, and wounded him, and departed, leaving him half dead.**

    v32 **And by chance there came down a certain priest that way:**

and when he saw him, he passed by on the other side.

v33 And likewise a Levite, when he was at the place, came and looked on him, and passed by on the other side.

v34 But a certain Samaritan, as he journeyed, came where he was: and when he saw him, he had compassion on him,

v35 And went to him, and bound up his wounds, pouring in oil and wine, and set him on his own beast, and brought him to an inn, and took care of him.

v36 And on the morrow when he departed, he took out two pence, and gave them to the host, and said unto him, Take care of him; and whatsoever thou spendest more, when I come again, I will repay thee."

The Levite and priest were high officials in the church. They were fellow countrymen to the injured man, distant family members, if you will. They were also supposed to be in the business of caring for the hurt and poor. It was part of their job.

Samaritans were highly despised by the Jews and the feeling was generally mutual. Yet in Jesus' story it was the despised one, the one the hurt man would have spit on if he could have, who helped him.

➢ Luke 10:36-37 **"Which now of these three, thinkest thou, was a _ _ _ _ _ _ _ _ unto him that fell among the _ _ _ _ _ _ _ ?' And he said, 'He that shewed _ _ _ _ _ on him.' Then said Jesus unto him, 'Go, and do thou likewise.'"**

I am to love other human beings as much as I love myself.

➢ Philippians 2:3-7 **"Let nothing be done through _ _ _ _ _ _ or _ _ _ _ _ _ _ _ _: but in lowliness of mind let each esteem other _ _ _ _ _ _ than themselves.**

v4 Look not every man on his own _ _ _ _ _ _, but every man also on the things of _ _ _ _ _ _.

4. What is the Character of God?

> **v5 Let this __ __ __ __ be in you which was also in __ __ __ __ __ __ __ __ __ __ __."**

Like Jesus, I am to put the needs of my fellow man ahead of my own needs. I am to serve others like Christ served them. This includes not only the people living in the physical house next door, but my spouse, my children, my parents and siblings, my friends and coworkers, my enemies and those on the other side of the planet.

If I have a Christ-like attitude, I will have Christ-like behavior.

God compares us to olive branches grafted into an olive trunk.

> Romans 11:17 **"And if some of the __ __ __ __ __ __ __ __ be broken off, and you, being a __ __ __ __ olive tree, were grafted in among them, and with them partake of the root and fatness of the olive tree;"**

When most trees are grafted onto a new trunk, they retain their original make up; an orange branch grafted onto a grapefruit trunk still produces oranges. A peach branch grafted onto an apricot trunk still produces peaches.

Olive trees are different. A wild olive branch grafted onto a domestic olive trunk will produce domestic olives. The branch becomes identical to the trunk.

The Bible says that Jesus is the trunk and we are the branches. When we accept His salvation, we become like Him.

Only by living a life of sacrifice can I have the fulfillment of truly knowing God. Only by following Luke 17:33 can I have true satisfaction.

> **"Whosoever shall seek to save his __ __ __ __ shall lose it; and whosoever shall __ __ __ __ his life shall __ __ __ __ __ __ __ __ it."**

I must lose my life to God in order to obtain true happiness.

5. Why Must I Get Saved?

Because I am a Sinner.

Because Adam disobeyed God in the Garden of Eden and ate of the forbidden fruit, sin became a part of my nature. I am not able to keep the commandments of God.

➢ Romans 5:12 "**Wherefore as by one man __ __ __ entered into the __ __ __ __ __, and death by sin; and so __ __ __ __ __ passed upon all men for that __ __ __ have __ __ __ __ __ __.**"

➢ Romans 3:23 "**For __ __ __ have __ __ __ __ __ __ and come short of the __ __ __ __ __ of God.**"

➢ Romans 6:23 "**For the __ __ __ __ __ of __ __ __ is __ __ __ __ __ …**"

➢ Ezekiel 18:20 "**The soul that __ __ __ __ __ __ __, it shall __ __ __ …**"

A sin is…

- Loving anything more than God
- Disrespecting my parents
- Having a selfish thought
- Pride
- Stealing
- Taking anything that is not mine
- Lying, deceit
- Lusting after someone who is not my spouse
- Adultery
- The misuse of sex
- Murder
- Hatred
- Violence
- Kidnapping
- Drunkenness
- Rebellion
- Being mean, unmerciful or unloving
- Stirring up trouble
- Not forgiving someone who hurts me
- Greed
- Gluttony
- Selfish anger
- Envy
- Gossip
- Cussing
- Worry
- Fear
- Witchcraft
- Breaking promises
- Being untrustworthy
- Not caring for the things we are supposed to take care of.
- Disobeying God
- Choosing to be stupid
- Stirring up Trouble
- Teaching false doctrines
- Being happy when others do the above
- Approving of other's sin [1]

---

[1] See Romans 1:21-32, Galatians 5:1-21, 1 Timothy 1:9-11, 2 Timothy 1:7, Exodus 20:3-17, Jeremiah 17:5, Matthew 6:14-15, Matthew 5:21-48, 1 John 2:9-11, 2:15-17, 3:7-10, 3:15, 4:18-21

5. Why Must I Get Saved?

It may help me to simply think of a sin as anything that does not please God.

➢ Jesus said, "For every __ __ __ __ is known by his own __ __ __ __ __." Luke 6:44

The above list is the fruit (sign) of sin. Sin cannot exist in the presence of God, so someone who sins cannot be with God.

All humans have sinned. It is not possible for any human to have not sinned. We simply aren't capable of being good by ourselves. This is because sin is just a sign of where my heart is. If my heart is trying to follow its own plan, I will sin.

Without salvation, my sin dooms me to hell, the Lake of Fire, eternal separation from God and all the good He has created. I deserve everlasting death.

God's Love for Me.

All my needs were provided for before I ever realized that I was a sinner.

Isaiah 53:5 tells me that Christ was "__ __ __ __ __ __ __ for my __ __ __ __ __ __ __ __ __ __ __ __ __ __, He was __ __ __ __ __ __ __ for my __ __ __ __ __ __ __ __ __ __: the chastisement of our __ __ __ __ __ __ was upon Him."

➢ 1 John 4:9, 10 "In this was manifested the __ __ __ __ of God toward us, because that God sent His only __ __ __ __ __ __ __ __ son into the world, that we might __ __ __ __ through Him.

v10 Herein is __ __ __ __ not that we loved __ __ __, but that He __ __ __ __ __ us, and __ __ __ __ His __ __ __ to be the Propitiation (atonement, payment) **for our sins.**"

➢ Jeremiah 31:3 "...Yea, I have loved thee with an __ __ __ __ __ __ __ __ __ __ __ love: therefore with loving-kindness have I __ __ __ __ __ __ thee."

21

5. Why Must I Get Saved?

Because I am not capable of being good enough to not sin or to pay for the sins I have committed, Jesus paid for my sins for me.

God's Provision for Me

➢ Isaiah 53:6 **"All we like __ __ __ __ __ have gone __ __ __ __ __ __; we have turned every one to his own __ __ __ and the Lord hath laid on Him** (Jesus) **the __ __ __ __ __ __ __ of us all."**

I am pictured as a lost sheep away from the shepherd. Christ the Good Shepherd sought me.

➢ Luke 19:10 **"For the Son of Man is come to __ __ __ __ and to __ __ __ __ that which was lost."**

➢ John 3:16 **"For God so __ __ __ __ __ the __ __ __ __ __ that He gave His __ __ __ __ begotten Son, that whosoever __ __ __ __ __ __ __ __ __ in Him should not perish but have everlasting life."**

I will reread John 3:16 (above) again putting my own name in place of the word "whosoever."

I hear the Good Shepherd's voice calling me and I will answer His call.

➢ Romans 5:8 **"But God commendeth His __ __ __ __ toward us, in that, while we were yet __ __ __ __ __ __ __, Christ died for us."**

Realizing this, I will repent (turn away from) my sins and confess with my mouth the Lord Jesus. I will respond to God's provision for me and receive forgiveness for my sins.

➢ 1 John 1:9 **"If we __ __ __ __ __ __ __ our sins, He is faithful and just to __ __ __ __ __ __ us our sins, and to __ __ __ __ __ __ __ us from all unrighteousness."**

I will take time now to accept Christ as my personal savior. If I am already saved, I will take this time to renew my commitment to the Lord.

"I have experienced something wonderful and supernatural since accepting Christ as my personal savior. Now I want a better understanding of what has taken place by studying the Bible. One thing I know: that He first loved me."

I Responded to God's Call.

Now that I've confessed Jesus and have accepted Him as my personal Savior, God dwells in me.

- 1 John 4:15 **"Whosoever shall __ __ __ __ __ __ __ that Jesus is the __ __ __ of God, __ __ __ dwelleth in him, and he in God."**

I am saved. All my sins have been erased.

- Romans 10:9-11 sates **"If thou shalt __ __ __ __ __ __ __ with thy __ __ __ __ __ the Lord Jesus, and shalt __ __ __ __ __ __ __ in thine heart that God hath raised Him from the dead, thou shalt be saved.**

    v10 **For with the __ __ __ __ __ man believeth unto __ __ __ __ __ __ __ __ __ __ __ __ __; and with the mouth confession is made unto __ __ __ __ __ __ __ __ __.**

    v11 **For the scripture saith, whosoever believeth on __ __ __ shall not be __ __ __ __ __ __."**

Now I am a part of God's family.

- John 1:12 **"But as many as __ __ __ __ __ __ __ __ Him, to them gave He power to become the __ __ __ __ of God, even to them that __ __ __ __ __ __ __ on His Name."**

I am Born of Him. I am His child.

- John 1:13 **"Which were __ __ __ __, not of __ __ __ __ __, nor of the will of the __ __ __ __ __ nor of the will of man, but of __ __ __."**

I was born once by physical birth of my earthly parents. Now I have a different birth through Christ.

5. Why Must I Get Saved?

➢ John 3:6 **"That which is born of the _ _ _ _ _ is _ _ _ _ _; and that which is born of the _ _ _ _ _ _ is _ _ _ _ _ _."**

With my human mind I can never understand the new birth for it is spiritual.

➢ 1 Corinthians 2:14 **"But the _ _ _ _ _ _ _ man receiveth not the things of the Spirit of God: for they are _ _ _ _ _ _ _ _ _ _ unto him: neither can he know them, because they are _ _ _ _ _ _ _ _ _ _ _ discerned."**

I know that I am a new creature.

➢ 2 Corinthians 5:17 **"Therefore if any man be in Christ, he is a new _ _ _ _ _ _ _ _: old things are passed away; behold, all things are become _ _ _."**

This change reminds me of the caterpillar, which is transformed into a beautiful butterfly. No longer is it an ugly crawling creature. Rather it has changed into a colorful flying one.

My life seems similar. God has changed my ugly sinful self, bound by habits of sin, into a person capable of exhibiting the Fruit of the Spirit; **"Love, joy, peace, longsuffering, (patience) gentleness, goodness, faith, meekness, temperance (self-control)."** Galatians 5:22, 23

My new birth is evidenced by my new motives, new desires, and a growing love for the things of God. My goal in life now is to be like Jesus.

➢ Ezekiel 36:26 **"A new _ _ _ _ _ also will I give you, and a new _ _ _ _ _ _ will I put within you…"**

So it is according to Titus 3:5

➢ **"Not by works of _ _ _ _ _ _ _ _ _ _ _ _ _ _ which we have done but according to His _ _ _ _ _ _ He saved us, by the _ _ _ _ _ _ _ of regeneration, and _ _ _ _ _ _ _ _ _ of the Holy Ghost."**

5. Why Must I Get Saved?

And since I have been (1 Peter 1:23) "__ __ __ __ **again, not of corruptible seed, but of incorruptible, by the __ __ __ __ of God, which liveth and abideth __ __ __ __ __ __ __.**" I now have eternal life.

➢ **"He that hath the Son hath Life."** 1 John 5:12

6. Assurance of Salvation

"And the work of righteousness shall be peace; and the effect of righteousness quietness and assurance forever." Isaiah 32:17

Assurance of salvation is for every child of God. Too many Christians are under a cloud of doubt unnecessarily because of not leaning on the sure Word of God.

My Need for Assurance

I need to know that I am saved because:

- I cannot depend on my feelings.
- I cannot depend on my works, keeping The Law, any set of rules in or out of the Bible, or any church tradition.
- I have an enemy, the devil, who lies to me about my salvation.

Therefore, I need assurance. God's Word provides this.

Positive Proofs of my Assurance

God's Word tells me that I am saved and that I can know it.

➢ John 3:36 **"He that __ __ __ __ __ __ __ __ __ on the Son hath everlasting __ __ __ __."**

➢ Romans 10:9 **"That if thou shalt confess with thy __ __ __ __ __ the Lord Jesus, and shalt __ __ __ __ __ __ __ in thine heart that God hath raised Him from the __ __ __ __, thou shalt be saved."**

I know by the witness of the Spirit of God.

➢ Romans 8:16 **"The __ __ __ __ __ __ itself beareth __ __ __ __ __ __ __ with our __ __ __ __ __ __, that we are the children of God."**

God has adopted me.

➢ Romans 8:15 **"For ye have not received the spirit of __ __ __ __ __ __ __ again to fear; but ye have received the spirit of**

6. Assurance of Salvation

_ _ _ _ _ _ _ _ **whereby we cry, Abba Father** (My Father)."

I know by my desire to do God's will and my new love for the brethren that I am saved.

- 1 John 4:13 **"Hereby know we that we _ _ _ _ _ in Him, and He in us, because He hath given us of His _ _ _ _ _ _."**

- 1 John 3:22 **"And whatsoever we ask, we _ _ _ _ _ _ _ of Him, because we keep His _ _ _ _ _ _ _ _ _ _ _ and do those things that are _ _ _ _ _ _ _ in His sight."**

- Romans 12:10 **"Be kindly _ _ _ _ _ _ _ _ _ _ _ one to another with brotherly love in _ _ _ _ _ preferring one _ _ _ _ _ _ _."**

I no longer seek the world's ways. Rather, I earnestly strive to apply Romans 12:2

"**And be not** _ _ _ _ _ _ _ _ _ **to this** _ _ _ _ _**: but be ye** _ _ _ _ _ _ _ _ _ _ **by the** _ _ _ _ _ _ _ **of your mind, that ye may prove what is that good, acceptable, and perfect** (mature) **will of God."**

I am Secure in Him

Christ has promised to keep me.

- Jude 24 **"Now unto him that is able to keep you from falling, and to present you _ _ _ _ _ _ _ _ before the presence of His glory with exceeding joy."**

- Romans 8:38, 39 **"For I am persuaded, that neither _ _ _ _ _, nor life, nor _ _ _ _ _ _, nor principalities, nor _ _ _ _ _ _, nor things present, nor things to _ _ _ _, nor height, nor _ _ _ _ _, nor any other creature, shall be able to _ _ _ _ _ _ _ _ us from the love of God, which is in Christ Jesus our Lord."**

6. Assurance of Salvation

The Bible says I have "Everlasting life."

➢ 1 John 5:13 **"These things have I written unto you that __ __ __ __ __ __ __ on the name of the Son of God; that ye may know that ye have __ __ __ __ __ __ __ life, and that ye may believe on the __ __ __ __ of the Son of God."**

➢ John 3:36 **"He that believeth on the __ __ __ hath everlasting __ __ __ __ : and he that believeth __ __ __ the Son shall not see life; but the __ __ __ __ __ of God abideth on him."**

How Does Someone know that he is saved.

How does a man know anything? By the evidence.

Suppose I am dealing with a friend who has accepted Christ, but has not the assurance, which a believer should have. Do I ask him to kneel down and pray until some happy feeling comes into his heart? No. I take God's Word and put it into his hand, and say, "My friend, will you read the 36th verse of the 3rd chapter of John?"

He reads *"He that __ __ __ __ __ __ __ __ __ on the Son hath everlasting __ __ __ __."*

I say to him "Who has everlasting life?"

"He that believes on the Son of God."

"Do you believe on the Son of God?"

"I do."

"Have you everlasting life?"

"No, I do not feel it."

I suggest that he reread the passage.

He reads, *"He that believeth on the Son hath everlasting life."*

I say, "Who hath everlasting life?"

He looks at the Book and says, *"He that believeth on the Son."*

"What have you?"

"Why, I do not know that I have anything."

"What does that verse say that the one who believes on the Son of God has? How many of those who believe on the Son have everlasting life?"

"All of them."

"How do you know it?"

"It says so."

"Do you believe on the Son?"

"I do."

"What have you?"

"Everlasting life."

"How do you know it?"

"Because God says so."

Satan's Response to My Salvation
> 1 Peter 5:8 "Be __ __ __ __ __, be __ __ __ __ __ __ __ __; because your adversary the __ __ __ __ __, as a roaring __ __ __ __, walketh about, seeking whom he may __ __ __ __ __ __."

Satan hates people and he wants as many as possible to join him in hell. He has had many centuries of practice at luring people away from God.

After I come to God, I will get sick, have surprise company, suffer a car breakdown, and many other events just at the perfect time to keep me from attending church.

All sorts of "fun" things that Christians aren't supposed to do will present themselves to me, usually with good friends or dear relatives begging me to join them.

Things will go wrong with my life to try to discourage me. I may lose my job, fight with my spouse or children, cars may break down. My health may suffer.

I may even have problems with other Christians; misunderstandings or different points of view.

If I hold true to God, though, in time He will give me the victory. I must abide in Him. This is like holding a small puppy in my hand; as long as the puppy sits still and content in my palm, he is safe. If he jumps off my hand, however, he will fall to the ground. I must determine I will serve Him no matter what. When I have proven this, Satan loses the power to annoy me.

➢ James 4:7b **"Resist the __ __ __ __ __ and he will __ __ __ __ from you."**

Can I Lose My Salvation?

Yes.

➢ Ezekiel 18:24 **"But when the __ __ __ __ __ __ __ __ __ turneth away from his righteousness, and committeth __ __ __ __ __ __ __ __, and doeth according to all the abominations that the __ __ __ __ __ __ man doeth, shall he __ __ __ __? All his __ __ __ __ __ __ __ __ __ __ __ __ __ that he hath done shall not be mentioned: in his __ __ __ __ __ __ __ __ that he hath trespassed, and in his __ __ __ that he hath __ __ __ __ __ __, in them shall he __ __ __."**

> 2 Peter 2:20,21 **"For if after they have escaped the pollutions of the _ _ _ _ _ through the knowledge of the Lord and Savior Jesus Christ, they are _ _ _ _ _ entangled therein, and overcome, the latter end is _ _ _ _ _ with them than the beginning.**

   v21 **For it had been better for them not to have _ _ _ _ _ the _ _ _ of righteousness, than, after they have known it, to _ _ _ _ from the _ _ _ _ commandment delivered unto them."**

It is possible for me to lose my salvation. However it isn't very likely. If I abide in Christ I shall live.

How do I know if I am backsliding?
I will know if I am backsliding if I begin to show the Fruits of the Flesh listed in Galatians 5:19-22:

"19 Now the works of the _ _ _ _ _ are manifest, which are these; Adultery, fornication, uncleanness, lasciviousness,

   v20 **Idolatry, witchcraft, _ _ _ _ _ _, variance, emulations, wrath, strife, seditions, heresies,**

   v21 **Envyings, murders, drunkenness, revellings, and such like: of the which I tell you before, as I have also told you in time past, that they which do such things shall _ _ _ inherit the kingdom of God."**

Or as worded in the New International Version:

19 The acts of the flesh are obvious: sexual immorality, impurity and debauchery;

20 idolatry and witchcraft; hatred, discord, jealousy, fits of rage, selfish ambition, dissensions, factions

21 and envy; drunkenness, orgies, and the like. I warn you, as I did before, that those who live like this will not inherit the kingdom of God.."

If these things begin to increase in my life, I am heading away from

God. There will come a time when I am so far away, I am no longer saved. I must keep a watch on myself to make sure I am always heading toward God. This path is obvious by the increase in the Fruits of the Spirit in my life:

Galatians 5 **"22 But the Fruit of the _ _ _ _ _ _ is love, joy, peace, long-suffering, gentleness, goodness, faith,**

v23 Meekness, temperance: against such there is no _ _ _.

v24 And they that are Christ's have _ _ _ _ _ _ _ _ _ the flesh with the affections and lusts.

v25 If we live in the Spirit, let us also _ _ _ _ in the Spirit.

v26 Let us not be desirous of _ _ _ _ glory, provoking one another, envying one another."

Or in the NIV:
22 But the fruit of the Spirit is love, joy, peace, forbearance, kindness, goodness, faithfulness,

23 gentleness and self-control. Against such things there is no law.

24 Those who belong to Christ Jesus have crucified the flesh with its passions and desires.

25 Since we live by the Spirit, let us keep in step with the Spirit.

26 Let us not become conceited, provoking and envying each other.

The Christian walk is a journey. As long as I am constantly showing more Fruits of the Spirit I am heading towards God. If I begin to show the Fruits of the Flesh instead, I have turned and headed the wrong way. I must repent (turn) and head to God again.

7. How Do I Discover God's Will?

"Wherefore be ye not unwise, but understanding what the will of the Lord is." Ephesians 5:17

God has a plan for this world and for my life. He wants me to know His will. If I ask and seek Him and study HIS WORD, He will make it known to me.

➢ Colossians 1:9 "…**That ye might be _ _ _ _ _ _ with the _ _ _ _ _ _ _ _ _ of His will in all _ _ _ _ _ _ and spiritual _ _ _ _ _ _ _ _ _ _ _ _ _.**"

I have a plan and a will of my own that I am in the habit of following (and will be tempted to follow for my whole life). Often it conflicts with what God would want for me. Therefore, I must pray "Your will be done."

Just like my pet dog is eager to please me and do whatever I am doing, I should be eager to please God. I should not have a cat-like attitude of independence and expecting God to please me.

Furthermore, I must earnestly listen for God's answer to my prayers and seek direction from the Bible.

➢ Proverbs 14:12 warns me **"There is a way which seemeth _ _ _ _ _ unto a man, but the ends thereof are the ways of death."**

➢ Jeremiah 17:9 **"The heart is _ _ _ _ _ _ _ _ _ above all things and desperately _ _ _ _ _ _. Who can know it?"**

I can't trust my own heart or emotions. That would be pursuing my own plans, not God's.

God desires for me to seek His purpose in my life.

➢ Romans 12:2 says "…**That ye may prove what is that _ _ _ _, and _ _ _ _ _ _ _ _ _ _, and _ _ _ _ _ _, will of**

God."

Since God knows everything and He loves me, it only makes logical sense for me to trust Him with every decision in every area of my life; to make Him my Boss. It would be highly illogical to not trust Him. I must ask if my desired course would please God according to His Word. Even if it is a hard path, obedience is worth it.

Is God part of my story…or am I part of God's story?

Ways by which I am guided into the will of God.
- His Word. Isaiah 40:8 **"…but the Word of our God shall _ _ _ _ _ for ever."**

All about me may change but God's Word won't! Any advice or direction that contradicts the Bible is not of God. He is not the Author of confusion and will not contradict Himself.

- His Spirit. Isaiah 30:21 **"…And thine ears shall _ _ _ _ a word behind thee, saying, _ _ _ _ is the way, _ _ _ _ ye in it when ye turn to the right hand, and when ye turn to the left."**

- Wait On The Lord. If I'm uncertain, what do I do? Pray. Do nothing. Make no decision because of a time limit. Unless I am sure it is God's leading, I will let the matter rest. Psalms 27:14 **"_ _ _ _ on the Lord; be of good _ _ _ _ _ _ _, and He shall strengthen thine _ _ _ _ _: _ _ _ _, I say, on the Lord."**

Above all, I don't worry. I can be concerned, but not fearful. I will remember that God is in charge and will work it all out.

> Romans 8:28 **"And we know that all _ _ _ _ _ _ work together for _ _ _ _ to them that love God, to them who are the called according to his _ _ _ _ _ _ _."**

Does this mean I won't ever suffer?
No. Sometimes God allows suffering;

- To build character in my life.

- Because of my own disobedience.
- Because there is a lesson I need to learn for my own growth that can only be learned through suffering.
- To help me understand someone else and their suffering so I can help them.
- Because we simply live in an imperfect world.

Whatever happens, I can trust that God is in control and nothing surprises Him. This trust is a sign of strength, not weakness. In the long run, anything that happens will be for the benefit of God's kingdom and thus for me.

Response-ability; Our Response to God's Ability

P-rayer
R-eleases
A-ll
Y-our
E-ternal
R-esources

Don't worry about anything, but pray about everything.

8. How to Overcome Temptation

Meeting the adversary's challenge and learning how to expose his lies.

Temptations Will Come

God wants me to live a life of righteousness, but even now that I belong to Jesus, I will have temptations. Christ knew this, so He said…

➢ Matthew 26:41 **"Watch and pray that ye enter not into _ _ _ _ _ _ _ _ _ _."**

The devil is the tempter. He will use every opportunity to try to trip me up.

➢ 1 Peter 5:8b pictures the devil **"as a roaring _ _ _ _ walking about, _ _ _ _ _ _ _ whom he may devour."**

Temptations also come because of my fleshly body. This is part of my heritage from Adam.

➢ James 1:14 **"But every man is _ _ _ _ _ _ _, when he is drawn away of his own _ _ _ _, and enticed."**

This applies not to just sexual lust, but to greed, pride, and desire for power and material gains.

➢ Romans 6:12,13 **"Let not _ _ _ therefore reign in your mortal body, that ye should obey it in the _ _ _ _ _ thereof. Neither _ _ _ _ _ ye your members** (of your bodies) **as instruments of _ _ _ _ _ _ _ _ _ _ _ _ _ _ unto sin: but yield yourselves unto _ _ _…"**

Nobody is perfect until they get to Heaven. We all make mistakes. But mistakes are different than sin (see the list of sin in the fifth chapter of this study.) A perfect, little green apple can still be perfect, though it is immature. As I get more mature in Christ, I will make fewer mistakes. I can still be sin free though I am not yet mature.

8. How to Overcome Temptation

I Can Overcome Temptations with God's Help
Christ is my example.

➢ Hebrews 4:15b **"But (Jesus) was in all points __ __ __ __ __ __ __ like as we are, yet without __ __ __."**

Christ's example was established when Satan tried to get Him to yield. See Matthew 4:1-11.

With each temptation Jesus answered the devil by saying. **"It is written…"**

I, too, need to rely on God's Word. 1 Corinthians 10:13 assures me that God does provide.

➢ **"There hath no __ __ __ __ __ __ __ __ __ __ taken you but such as is common to man: but God is __ __ __ __ __ __ __ __ who will not suffer you to be __ __ __ __ __ __ __ above that ye are able; but will with the temptation also make a way to __ __ __ __ __ __ that ye may be able to bear it."**

Strength comes from God who cannot be tempted.

➢ James 1:13 **"Let no man say when he is tempted, 'I am tempted of __ __ __:' for God cannot be tempted with __ __ __ __, neither __ __ __ __ __ __ __ __ He any man."**

I must recognize that temptations are from the devil.

➢ James 4:7 **"__ __ __ __ __ __ yourselves therefore to God. __ __ __ __ __ __ the devil, and he will __ __ __ __ from you."**

I am not to **"give place to the devil."** Ephesians 4:27

When tempting thoughts come into my mind, I should dismiss those thoughts and replace them with scripture or praise to God. Christ helps me.

➢ Philippians 4:13 **"I can do __ __ __ __ __ __ __ __ __ through Christ which strengtheneth me."**

➢ Hebrews 2:18 **"He is able to succor** (give aid to) **them that are** _ _ _ _ _ _ _**."**

What if I yield to Temptation?
1 John 3:8 **"He that** _ _ _ _ _ _ _ _ _ _ **sin is of the** _ _ _ _ _**"**

Jesus said to **"…Go, and sin no more."** John 8:11

If I live a lifestyle of sin, I am not saved. However, if I slip up and yield on one occasion, I am still in the family of God, but in need of repentance.

I will not be defeated and despondent. I'll recall…

➢ Psalm 119:9 **"Wherewithal shall a young man** _ _ _ _ _ _ _ **his way? By taking heed thereto according to thy** _ _ _ _**."**

Strength will be mine for I'm assured in 1 John 1:9 that

➢ **"… if we** _ _ _ _ _ _ _ **our sins, He is faithful and just to** _ _ _ _ _ _ _ **us our sins, and to** _ _ _ _ _ _ _ **us from all unrighteousness."**

I will go immediately in prayer to ask forgiveness for my failure.

I'll remember that (2 Peter 2:9) **"The Lord knoweth how to deliver the** _ _ _ _ _ **out of temptations, and to reserve the** _ _ _ _ _ _ **unto the day of judgment to be punished."**

After having confessed my sins, I'll strive to…

➢ Ephesians 6:10 **"… Be** _ _ _ _ _ _ **in the Lord, and in the** _ _ _ _ _ **of His might."**

How do I do this?
Ephesians 6:11-18 tells me to **"Put on the whole** _ _ _ _ _ **of God, that ye may be able to stand against the wiles of the** _ _ _ _ _**.**

8. How to Overcome Temptation

v12 **For we _ _ _ _ _ _ _ not against flesh and blood, but against principalities, against _ _ _ _ _ _, against the rulers of the _ _ _ _ _ _ _ _ of this world, against _ _ _ _ _ _ _ _ _ wickedness in high places.**

v13 **Wherefore take unto you the whole armor of God, that ye may be able to _ _ _ _ _ _ _ _ _ in the evil day, and having done all to stand,**

v14 **_ _ _ _ _ therefore, having your loins girt about with _ _ _ _ _ and having on the breastplate of _ _ _ _ _ _ _ _ _ _ _.**

v15 **And you feet shod with the preparation of the _ _ _ _ _ _ of _ _ _ _ _;**

v16 **Above all, taking the shield of _ _ _ _ _, wherewith ye shall be able to quench all the fiery darts of the wicked.**

v17 **And take the helmet of _ _ _ _ _ _ _ _ _ and the _ _ _ _ _ of the spirit, which is the Word of God.**

v18 **_ _ _ _ _ _ _ always with all prayer and supplication in the Spirit, and _ _ _ _ _ _ _ _ thereunto with all perseverance and supplication for all saints."**

Prayer, Bible reading and Fellowship with other Christians will help me to resist temptation. As I become more mature in God, more Christ-like, I will recognize temptations sooner and be able to resist them better.

I will memorize some scripture verses related to overcoming temptations such as…

1 Corinthians 10:13
Philippians 4:13
2 Peter 2:9

…so that when I am tempted I can quote God's word as Jesus did when He was tempted and say, **"It is written…"**

Three Major Temptations of a Christian's Life
1. Youth- the wolf of lust.
2. Middle Age- the tiger of pride, success, status and position.
3. Old Age- the lion of financial security.

Temptations Can Bring Joy
Temptations are testing with the intent of creating spiritual good. They are the trying of my faith. Read Genesis 22:1-18, the account of God testing Abraham's faith.

- James 1:2-4 "My brethren, count it all __ __ __ when ye fall into divers temptations; Knowing this, that the trying of your __ __ __ __ __ worketh __ __ __ __ __ __ __ __. But let patience have her perfect work that ye may be __ __ __ __ __ __ __ and entire, wanting nothing."

- James 1:12 "Blessed is the man that endureth __ __ __ __ __ __ __ __ __: for when he is tried he shall receive the __ __ __ __ __ of life, which the Lord hath promised to them that love Him."

9. Learning To Pray

Prayer is my spiritual lifeline.

Jesus is my mediator and High Priest. Through Jesus I have direct access to God.

> 1 Timothy 2:5 **"For there is one ___ ___ ___ and one ___ ___ ___ ___ ___ ___ ___ ___ between God and men, the man ___ ___ ___ ___ ___ ___ ___ ___ ___ ___ ___."**

Prayer is an expression of my needs, and God invites me to ask even though He already knows what my needs are.

> Luke 11:9 **"... Ask, and it shall be ___ ___ ___ ___ ___ you; seek, and ye shall ___ ___ ___ ___; knock, and it shall be ___ ___ ___ ___ ___ ___ unto you."**

It is also the time and way to fight Satan and his influence in my life and the lives of those I love.

> Matthew 17:21 **"However, this kind goes not out but by ___ ___ ___ ___ ___ ___ and ___ ___ ___ ___ ___ ___ ___."**

"Fasting" is when I devote the time I would normally spend eating to prayer instead. Most of the time this means a complete absence of eating, though some have "fasted" by giving up one favorite item (such as French Fries or all sugar) for a time. Some pick one day a week or a month to fast as a gift to God. Fasting gives extra power to my prayers and discipline to my life.

What do I pray about?

Everything.

God wants to be involved in every area of my life.

> Philippians 4:6 **"Be careful for nothing;** ("Don't be worried about anything." Living Letters Bible) **but in everything by ___ ___ ___ ___ ___ ___ and ___ ___ ___ ___ ___ ___ ___ ___ ___ ___ ___ with thanksgiving let your ___ ___ ___ ___ ___ ___ ___ ___ be made known unto God."**

9. Learning to Pray

I will be earnest and sincere as God knows and sees my heart before He hears my words.

Why Pray?

God designed the universe to respond to my prayers. The Bible is full of examples of God actually changing His mind when His people pray.

- When God was going to destroy Israel for their whining, Moses begged Him not to and He didn't.

- When they ran out of wine at the wedding in Canaan, Mary asked Jesus to do something about it. He originally refused, but because of her faith and acts of obedience, He ended up creating wine for the celebration.

These are just two examples.

Prayer is a form of worship. As a child of God it is my privilege to go directly to God with my needs, my requests, and my Thanksgiving.

➢ John 4:24 **"God is a __ __ __ __ __ __; and they that worship Him must __ __ __ __ __ __ __ Him in __ __ __ __ __ __ and in __ __ __ __ __ __."**

It develops a habit of close fellowship with God.

It preserves me from evil.

➢ Matthew 6:13 **"And lead us not into __ __ __ __ __ __ __ __ __ __, but deliver us from __ __ __ __..."**

It brings forgiveness.

➢ 1 John 1:9 **"If we confess our sins He is __ __ __ __ __ __ __ __ and just to __ __ __ __ __ __ __ us our sins…"**

It secures me, strengthens me, and gives me personal guidance.

It can cause my loved ones to get saved. The Bible says that it is God's will for everyone to be saved.

Jesus told His disciples to:

> Matthew 9:38 "__ __ __ __ you therefore the Lord of the __ __ __ __ __ __ __, that He will send forth __ __ __ __ __ __ __ __ into His harvest."

God has set up the universe so that the very elements are moved by the prayers of the saints. My prayers are powerful and DO change things.

Different kinds of Prayer

SINNER'S PRAYER
God is waiting and will always hear and answer the prayer of repentance from the heart of the sinner.

> 1 Timothy 2:4 "Who will have __ __ __ men to be __ __ __ __ __, and to come unto the __ __ __ __ __ __ __ __ of the __ __ __ __ __."

> Acts 2:21 "Whosoever shall __ __ __ __ on the name of the Lord shall be __ __ __ __ __."

PRAYER FOR HELP IN TROUBLE.
Psalm 22:11 "Be not __ __ __ from me; for trouble is near; for there is none to help."

> Matthew 14:30 "But when he (Peter) saw the wind boisterous, (and that he was sinking in the waves) he was afraid; and beginning to sink, he __ __ __ __ __, saying 'Lord __ __ __ __ me.'"

PRAYER OF THANKSGIVING.
Ephesians 5:20 "Giving thanks __ __ __ __ __ __ for all things unto God and the Father in the name of our Lord Jesus Christ."

> 1 Thessalonians 5:18 "In __ __ __ __ __ __ __ __ __ __ give thanks..."

9. Learning to Pray

INTERCESSORY PRAYER- INTERSESSORY PRAYER
Prayer on the behalf of others.

Christ prayed for his disciples.

➢ John 17:9-10 "I __ __ __ __ for them: I pray not for the __ __ __ __ __, but for them which thou hast given me; for they are thine. And all mine are thine, and thine are mine; and I am __ __ __ __ __ __ __ __ in them."

Abraham prayed for the righteous in Sodom, the wicked city. Geneses 18:20-32

Moses prayed for the children of Israel.

➢ Deuteronomy 9:18 "And I fell down before the LORD, as at the __ __ __ __ __, forty days and forty nights: I did neither eat bread, nor drink water, because of all your __ __ __ __ which ye sinned, in doing wickedly in the sight of the LORD, to __ __ __ __ __ __ __ him to anger."

The disciples and early church prayed for Peter while he was in prison.

➢ Acts 12:5 "Peter therefore was kept in prison: but __ __ __ __ __ __ was made without __ __ __ __ __ __ __ of the church unto God for him."

LONG PRAYERS
Strength in prayer is better than length.

➢ Matthew 6:7 warns "But when ye __ __ __ __, use not vain repetitions, as the heathen do; for they think that they shall be __ __ __ __ __ for their much speaking."

Long prayers are not required, but are ok if I feel I need to spend extra time in prayer with God.

9. Learning to Pray

> Matthew 6:8 "... For your Father __ __ __ __ __ __ __ what things ye have __ __ __ __ of, before ye ask Him."

PUBLIC PRAYERS
When I am asked to pray in public, I must remember that I am praying to God and leading others to His throne of grace.

INSINCERE OR SELFISH PRAYERS
Some prayers are not heard because of sin in my life.

> Psalm 66:18 "If I regard __ __ __ __ __ __ __ __ in my heart, the Lord will __ __ __ hear me."

Some prayers are unanswered because I've asked selfishly.

> James 4:3 "Ye __ __ __, and receive not, because ye ask __ __ __ __ __, that ye may consume it upon your __ __ __ __ __."

Some prayers, however, are answered, but God says "No," or "Wait." Since He knows everything and loves me, I must trust that these answers are the right ones for me and my life.

PRIVATE MATTERS.
> Matthew 6:6 "But thou, when thou __ __ __ __ __ __ __ enter into thy __ __ __ __ __ __, and when thou hast shut thy door, __ __ __ __ to thy Father which is in __ __ __ __ __ __; and thy Father which seeth in secret shall reward thee __ __ __ __ __ __;"

UNSPOKEN PRAYERS.
> 1 Samuel 1:13 "Hannah __ __ __ __ __ __ for a son, she spake in her heart; only her lips moved, but her voice was not __ __ __ __ __."

> Hebrews 4:12 "For the word of God is .... a discerner of the __ __ __ __ __ __ __ __ and __ __ __ __ __ __ __ of the heart.

How often do I pray?
If I love someone, I don't ask, "How often should I talk with them."

9. Learning to Pray

- Luke 18:1 "...men ought _ _ _ _ _ _ to pray and not to faint."
- 1 Thessalonians 5:17 **"Pray without _ _ _ _ _ _ _."**

  I will try to at least begin and end my day with prayer.

How do I begin?

I will address my prayer to my Heavenly Father with respect and a proper title, even as Christ set the example for me.

- Matthew 6:9 **"Our Father Who art in Heaven, _ _ _ _ _ _ _ _ be Thy Name..."**

  Some titles might be:

Our Father,	Gracious Father in Heaven,	Jesus, or even Daddy Father (Abba Father);
My Heavenly Father,		
Dear Heavenly Father,	Our Loving God,	
	Dear God	

Anything that shows respect and love for God. See the list of names for God in chapter 4 of this workbook.

What should my prayer include?

1. Adoration And Praise - Example; The Book of Psalms. Praising God is always appropriate, but especially before making requests. I can use the list of the names of God, quote praise Psalms, or just use my own words.

2. Thanksgiving and outpouring of gratitude to God because of His grace, mercy and loving kindness. Example; Psalms 103:1-2 **"Bless the LORD, O my soul: and all that is within me, _ _ _ _ _ His holy name. _ _ _ _ _ the LORD, O my soul, and forget not all His benefits: ..."**

3. Communion with God. Example; Luke 6:12 **"And it came to pass in those days, that He went out into a mountain to _ _ _ _, and continued all night in _ _ _ _ _ _ to God."**

- 1 John 1:3 **"That which we have seen and heard _ _ _ _ _ _ _ we unto you, that ye also may have fellowship with us: and truly**

our fellowship is ____ the Father, and ____ His Son Jesus

4. Confession of Sins and Wrongs. Example; Psalms 51 **"Have _____ upon me, O God, according to Thy lovingkindness: … v3 For I acknowledge my transgressions: and my ___ is ever before me.**

   ➢ v4 **Against Thee, Thee only, have I _____, and done this evil in Thy sight:…**

   ➢ v10 **Create in me a _____ heart, O God; and renew a _____ spirit within me…. _____ me from bloodguiltiness, O God, Thou God of my salvation: and my tongue shall sing aloud of Thy righteousness. …**

   ➢ v17 **The sacrifices of God are a _____ spirit: a broken and a _____ heart, O God, Thou wilt not despise…."**

5. Petitions (plea for personal help). Example; Romans 9:1-2 **"I say the truth in Christ, I lie not, my conscience also bearing me witness in the Holy Ghost, That I have great _____ and continual _____ in my heart."**

   ➢ Matthew 6 4 **"That thine alms may be in _____: and thy Father which seeth in secret Himself shall _____ thee openly."**

   ➢ Philippians 4:6 **"Be careful for _____; but in every thing by _____ and supplication with _____ let your requests be made known unto God."**

6. Intercession. Example: Romans 10:1 **"Brethren, my heart's desire and _____ to God for Israel is, that they might be saved."**

7. Submission. Example: Luke 22:42 **"Saying, Father, if thou be _____, remove this cup from me: nevertheless ___ my will, but _____, be done."**

The sample prayer Jesus gave to us:

➤ Matthew 6:9 **"After this manner therefore pray ye** (Not after the words necessarily. "In this way."**):**

➤ **"Our __ __ __ __ __ __ which art in heaven,** (I will acknowledge who I am talking to.)

➤ __ __ __ __ __ __ __ __ **be thy name** (I will praise Him).

➤ **Thy kingdom come, Thy will be done in __ __ __ __ __, as it is in heaven** (I will pray for God's will to be done, first of all in my home, then my block, neighborhood, town, state, country and the world. I will pray for my neighbors, friends and family by name. I will include my pastor and my president.)

➤ __ __ __ __ **us this day our daily bread** (I will now ask for those things I and others need. I will keep a list of prayer requests [in my Daily Planner?] that I will go over every day. I don't have to go on and on about these needs though. God knows them and I have faith in my prayers that He is answering them.).

➤ **And __ __ __ __ __ __ __ us our debts, as we forgive our debtors** (Sin creates a debt. I must ask God to forgive me for those sins I have committed. If I also truly forgive those who have sinned against me, who have harmed me, who have offended me, God WILL forgive my offenses against Him.).

➤ **And __ __ __ __ us not into temptation, but __ __ __ __ __ __ __ us from evil:** (It is ok to ask to not be tempted by sin. I pray this for my children as well as myself regularly. I also pray that God lets me catch them when they do begin to sin and to have the wisdom to correct them in the most effective way to produce righteousness.)

➤ **For thine is the kingdom, and the __ __ __ __ __, and the __ __ __ __ __, for ever** (I will acknowledge His power).

➤ **Amen** (so be it)."

9. Learning to Pray

Conditions upon which prayer avails

• Prayer must be in faith. Hebrews 11:6 "But without __ __ __ __ __ it is impossible to please Him: for he that cometh to God must __ __ __ __ __ __ __ that He is, and that He is a rewarder of them that diligently __ __ __ __ Him.

Matthew 17:20 "And Jesus said unto them, 'Because of your __ __ __ __ __ __ __ __: for verily I say unto you, If ye have __ __ __ __ __ __ as a grain of mustard seed, ye shall say unto this mountain, Remove hence to yonder place; and it __ __ __ __ __ remove; and nothing shall be __ __ __ __ __ __ __ __ __ unto you.'"

Mark 11:23-24 "For verily I say unto you, That __ __ __ __ __ __ __ __ __ shall say unto this mountain, Be thou __ __ __ __ __ __ __, and be thou cast into the sea; and shall not __ __ __ __ __ __ in his heart, but shall __ __ __ __ __ __ __ that those things which he saith shall come to pass; he shall have __ __ __ __ __ __ __ __ __ __ he saith. Therefore I say unto you, What things soever ye desire, when ye pray, __ __ __ __ __ __ __ that ye receive them, and ye shall __ __ __ __ them."

• Pray in the name (Authority) Of Jesus. John 14:13 "And whatsoever ye shall ask in My __ __ __ __, that will I do, that the Father may be __ __ __ __ __ __ __ __ __ in the Son."

John 15:16 "Ye have not chosen Me, but I have __ __ __ __ __ __ you, and __ __ __ __ __ __ __ __ you, that ye should go and bring forth __ __ __ __ __ __, and that your fruit should remain: that __ __ __ __ __ __ __ __ __ __ ye shall ask of the Father in My Name, He may __ __ __ __ __ it you."

• Prayer should be made under direction and dynamic of the Holy Spirit. Jude 1:20 "But ye, beloved, building up yourselves on your most holy faith, __ __ __ __ __ __ __ in the __ __ __ __ __ __ __ __ __ __."

9. Learning to Pray

- Sin must be confessed and renounced. Psalms 66:18 **"If I regard iniquity in my __ __ __ __ __, the Lord will __ __ __ hear me:"**

    Isaiah 59:1-2 **"Behold, the LORD's hand is not __ __ __ __ __ __ __ __ __, that it cannot __ __ __ __; neither His __ __ __ heavy, that it cannot __ __ __ __: But your iniquities have __ __ __ __ __ __ __ __ between you and your God, and your __ __ __ __ __ have hid His face from you, that He will not __ __ __ __."**

    Sin separates us from God.

- I must have a forgiving heart. Mark 11:25-26 **"And when ye stand praying, __ __ __ __ __ __ __, if ye have ought against any: that your Father also which is in heaven may __ __ __ __ __ __ __ you your trespasses. But if ye do not forgive, __ __ __ __ __ __ __ will your Father which is in heaven forgive __ __ __ __ trespasses."**

- My prayer should be in keeping with the will of God. 1 John 5:14-15 **"And this is the confidence that we have in Him, that, if we ask __ __ __ thing according to His __ __ __ __, He heareth us: And if we know that He hear us, __ __ __ __ __ __ __ __ __ we ask, we know that we have the petitions that we desired of Him."**

How do I close my prayer?
By giving recognition to Jesus Christ as our Father and Lord.

- In The Name (Authority) Of Jesus. John 14:13 **"And whatsoever ye shall __ __ __ in My Name, that will I do, that the Father may be glorified in the __ __ __."**

    God has given His Son authority.

    Ephesians 1:22 **"And hath put __ __ __ things under His feet, and gave Him to be the __ __ __ __ over all things to the church."**

    Sample: "Thank you for the answer, Father. Amen."

- Amen. This means "So be it." It indicates our willingness to accept God's answer whether yes or no.

Question: Should you close your prayer or continue in a mind of prayer all day?

10. How to Read the Bible
The Bible is God's Love-Letter to Me

The Instruction Book

God's direct will and instruction for me is in His Word; the Bible.

As a plane in flight needs a chart and instruction from the tower, so I need to know God's Word for instruction and direction for my life.

➢ Romans 15:4 **"For whatsoever things were written aforetime were written for our __ __ __ __ __ __ __, that we through patience and comfort of the __ __ __ __ __ __ __ __ __ might have hope."**

To keep my direction clear and stay on the Christian course I must know God's Word.

➢ Psalm 119:15 **"Thy word is a __ __ __ __ unto my feet, and a __ __ __ __ __ unto my path."**

The Bible is the light for my way.

➢ Psalms 119:11 **"Thy __ __ __ __ have I hid in mine heart that I might not __ __ __ against thee."**

God has given His Word in a supernatural way.

➢ 2 Timothy 3:16 **"All __ __ __ __ __ __ __ __ __ is given by inspiration of God and is profitable for __ __ __ __ __ __ __ __, for __ __ __ __ __ __ __, for __ __ __ __ __ __ __ __ __, for instruction in __ __ __ __ __ __ __ __ __ __ __ __ __."**

- Doctrine shows me the path to follow.
- Reproof shows me when I am off the path.
- Correction shows me how to get back on the path.
- Instruction in righteousness shows me how to stay on the path.

➢ 2 Peter 1:21 **"For the prophecy (Word) came not in old time by the will of __ __ __, but holy men of __ __ __ spake as they were moved by the __ __ __ __ __ __ __ __ __."**

10. How to Read the Bible

Bible Reading Provides Food For My New Spiritual Nature.
As a newborn spiritual babe I should...

➢ 1 Peter 2:2 "... **Desire the sincere __ __ __ __ of the Word...**"

I need to feed my spiritual nature and partake of God's Word as much as possible in order to grow.

➢ Matthew 4:4 "**Man shall not live by __ __ __ __ __ alone, but by every __ __ __ __ that proceedeth out of the mouth of God.**"

➢ Jeremiah 15:16 "**Thy __ __ __ __ __ were found, and I did __ __ __ them; and Thy Word was unto me the __ __ __ and rejoicing of mine heart;...**"

➢ 2 Timothy 2:15 "**__ __ __ __ __ to show thyself approved unto God, a workman that needeth not to be ashamed, rightly dividing the __ __ __ __ of truth.**"

I will study the Bible so God will approve of my work because I truly understand His will in my life.

Bible Reading Provides My Strength.
Reading and knowing the scriptures is the key to overcoming sin and living a victorious Christian life.

➢ Ephesians 6:17 admonishes me to "**Take the __ __ __ __ __ __ of salvation, and the __ __ __ __ __ of the spirit, which is the __ __ __ __ of God.**"

The Bible is my most effective tool to use in my Christian walk and warfare against the devil; It is my only offensive weapon.

➢ Hebrews 4:12 "**For the Word of God is __ __ __ __ __ and __ __ __ __ __ __ __ __, and sharper than any two-edged sword, piercing even to the dividing asunder of __ __ __ and __ __ __ __ __ __, and of the joints and marrow, and is a discerner of the __ __ __ __ __ __ __ __ and __ __ __ __ __ __ of the heart.**"

53

Biblical Interpretation

Proper understanding of the Bible requires three basic tools;
- understanding of biblical context,
- understanding of historical context, and
- understanding of original languages.

In order to understand scripture I must always take the context of scripture into account. What was the author saying in the whole chapter, the whole book? Who was he talking to? Why?

There once was a man who wanted to know God's will in his life. He randomly opened his Bible. It fell to the scripture where Judas killed himself. Wondering what this meant for him, he randomly opened his Bible again. This time it fell open to Luke 10:37 "**...Then said Jesus unto him, Go, and do thou likewise.**" Was this God telling him to kill himself? Of course not. I must take scripture in its context. I cannot take a verse here and a verse there and put them together to form a belief. This is mishandling of the Word of God.

God tells some people to do things He doesn't want everyone to do. For example, all believers are not to go preach to Nineveh as Jonah was told to do. Nor build a large boat and gather a bunch of animals onto it. Nor lay in the middle of the city, naked, eating nothing but bread and not talking for an entire year like Ezekiel was told to do. I must pay attention to who each scripture was written to and why. The moral lessons taught in every scripture can be applied to my life, but the fact of the scripture applies to who it was written to. This becomes clearer every time I read through the scriptures.

The second rule of biblical interpretation requires I see what was happening in history. For example, when God told Jonah to go to Nineveh (the capital of the Assyrian empire), it was because the Ninavites were very cruel conquerors of the entire region. They would cut the heads off of the leaders of each city-state they conquered and often torture the inhabitants. God was fed up. He sent Jonah to warn them to change their ways- or else. Of course I know that it worked; they repented and God spared the city. Well, for a while anyway. History tells me that the city relapsed into its old ways and was destroyed for its cruelty a generation or so later.

I must understand the history surrounding an event to truly understand what the Bible is telling me. Again, this becomes clearer as I become more familiar with the Word. After I have become more familiar, a good history book or study guide can help me learn the history of the time. There are even some Bibles that are combined with history books so I can have both at once.

The third tool I need to really understand the Bible is a knowledge of original languages. This is not so hard as it used to be. Any Internet-connected computer has access to a Strong's Concordance (and they are available in book-form from any book seller for as little as $10.00). This is a list of each word in the Bible and its location AND its definition in the original language. I simply look up the words in a verse and see what the original author meant.

Instructions for reading the Bible

I will read the Bible regularly (daily) for:

- Spiritual food and strength.
- Learning more of God and His plan for mankind.
- Pleasure and blessing I receive in my newfound life in Christ.
- Discovering God's promises and deeper truths.

I will read it slowly with a prayerful attitude and open mind.
I will read it where I can concentrate.
I will enjoy what I do understand and leave portions I do not understand until I am more fully acquainted with the Bible and more spiritually mature. I will understand more every time I read it.

I will...

•Read the New Testament through first; then, read some out of both Testaments, a chapter or two out of each every day.

•Read it from cover to cover get the general overall view of God's Word.

•Read the life of Jesus Christ (the four gospels: Matthew, Mark, Luke and John).

•Read about the Early Church (Acts, the two epistles of Peter, the three epistles of John). **Or**...

10. How to Read the Bible

- Find out the areas I wish to pursue more deeply and use the concordance to help me find relevant scriptures.

I will take the Bible at face value, believe it means what it says, and is not written in riddles or codes. God's purpose for giving me the Bible was to help me understand Him, not to confuse or mystify me.

I will memorize at least one verse every week; starting with my favorites. There is often a list of good verses to memorize in the back of the Bible, plus the Internet has many such lists (Search for "Bible memory verse list"). A box or set of cards called "Precious Promises" or "Daily Bread" is available for purchase at almost any Bible bookstore and may be helpful. Or I can buy Betty Tracy's book "Thy Word Have I Hidden," which has at least one memory verse from each book of the Bible[2].

➢ **"Forever, O Lord, Thy Word is settled in heaven."** Psalm 119:89

➢ **"The grass withereth, the flower fadeth; but the Word of our God shall stand forever."** Isaiah 40:8

Scriptures to read

- When in sorrow, I'll read John 14.
- When men fail me, I'll read Psalm 27.
- When I have sinned, I'll read Psalm 51.
- When I worry, I'll read Matthew 6:19-34.
- When I am in danger, I'll read Psalm 91.
- When I have the blues, I'll read Psalm 34.
- When God seems far away, I'll read Psalm 139.
- When I am discouraged, I'll read Isaiah 40.
- If I want to be fruitful, I'll read John 15.
- When doubts come upon me, I'll read John 7:17.
- When I am lonely or fearful, I'll read Psalm 23.
- When I forget my blessings, I'll read Psalm 103.
- For Jesus' idea of a Christian, I'll read Matthew 5.
- For James' idea of religion, I'll read James 1:19-27.

---

[2] Available at http://TheBettysBooks.com

- When my faith needs stirring, I'll read Hebrews 11.
- When I feel down and out, I'll read Romans 8:31-39
- When I want courage for my task, I'll read Joshua 1.
- When the world seems bigger than God, I'll read Psalm 90.
- When I want rest and peace, I'll read Matthew 11:25-30.
- When I want Christian assurance, I'll read Romans 8:1-30.
- For Paul's idea of Christianity, I'll read 2 Corinthians 5:15-19.
- For Paul's rules on how to get along with men, I'll read Romans 12.

I will follow Psalm 119:11 and hide some of these in my memory.

The Bible is the most important document ever written. It is the inspired word of God. God dictated it to righteous men:

➢ 2 Peter 1:21 **"For the __ __ __ __ __ __ __ __ came not in old time by the will of __ __ __: but holy men of God __ __ __ __ __ as they were moved by the __ __ __ __ __ __ __ __ __."**

➢ 2 Timothy 3:16 **"All scripture is given by inspiration of __ __ __, and is profitable for doctrine, for reproof, for correction, for instruction in righteousness."**

Without the Bible we cannot know God. It tells us of His character and His will in the world and in our lives.

It is also the foundation for our Western Society, American government, and our culture.

It is the greatest piece of literature ever written containing some of the most beautiful prose and poetry ever written (Psalms, as well as many individual passages, rhyme in Hebrew).

It is essential that we study our Bible regularly. We cannot become too familiar with it. Though biblical knowledge doesn't always mean Christian maturity, this is how we draw closer to God.

11. Facts About The Bible

The Bible is made up of 66 books: 39 from the Old Testament and 27 from the New.

The Old Testament has thirty-nine books (Memory help: there are three letters in the word "old" and nine in the word "testament"= 39).

The first five are called the Pentateuch, and most attribute them to Moses. They are:
- Genesis (Creation through the life of Joseph)
- Exodus (The Israelites leaving Egypt and traveling to the promised land)
- Leviticus (Various laws given by God)
- Numbers (The numbering of Israel and various laws)
- Deuteronomy (Various Laws)

The next twelve are the books of history. They are:
- Joshua (written by Joshua telling of Israel's conquering of the promised land)
- Judges (The history of Israel under the rule of judges, from Joshua to Samuel)
- Ruth (A romance story)
- 1 Samuel (The birth of Samuel, crowning of Saul as the first king)
- 2 Samuel (The story of David and Saul)
- 1Kings (The history of Judah and Israel, from a kingly perspective, from Solomon to the captivity)
- 2 Kings (The history of Judah and Israel, from a kingly perspective, from Solomon to the captivity)
- 1 Chronicles (The history of Judah and Israel, from a priestly perspective, from Solomon to the captivity)
- 2 Chronicles (The history of Judah and Israel, from a priestly perspective, from Solomon to the captivity)
- Ezra (Israel returns to Jerusalem after the Babylonian Captivity.)
- Nehemiah (Israel returns to Jerusalem after the Babylonian Captivity.)
- Ester (A story of God's provision and protection, though the book does not use the name of God anywhere at all.)

Then come the books of poetry:
- Job (The trials of a righteous man and a debate about the nature of

God.)
- Psalms (Songs)
- Proverbs (Wise sayings)
- Ecclesiastics (The purpose of life)
- Song of Songs (or Solomon; a love story)

<u>The Major Prophets (each written by the man the book is named after):</u>
- Isaiah (Tells of the coming destruction of many countries as well as the ending history of Judah.)
- Jeremiah (Tells of the coming destruction of Judah and of its actual end. He was in the city at the time it happened.)
- Lamentations (written by Jeremiah to mourn the death of the king.)
- Ezekiel (many prophecies from the end of Judah to the coming of Christ.)
- Daniel (the story of the Captivity and prophecies concerning the rest of the history of the Israelite people).

<u>And the Minor Prophets (each written by the man the book is named after):</u>
- Hosea (Prophecy of the coming Assyrian Captivity and an example of God's love for Israel.)
- Joel (A description of a coming plague, a call to repentance, and prophecy of the coming Messiah.)
- Amos (The shepherd prophet; coming judgment on Israel's enemies and Israel herself. A call to repentance.)
- Obadiah (Judgment pronounced on Edom.)
- Jonah (A story about rebellion and redemption.)
- Micah (The story of Israel's sin, judgment and restoration.)
- Nahum (Nineveh is doomed.)
- Habakkuk (Prophecy of Judah's destruction.)
- Zephaniah (Prophecy of Israel's destruction and restoration.)
- Haggai (An exhortation for the restored Israel to finish the Temple.)
- Zechariah (Prophecy of the coming Messiah and His work.)
- Malachi (God's answers to man's questions. A call to righteousness.)

The New Testament has twenty-seven books (Memory help: three letters in the word "new" times nine letters in the word "testament" equals twenty-seven.)

<u>The first four books are about the life of Christ, and are named after the authors and are called the Gospels:</u>
- Matthew (From the Hebrew perspective.)
- Mark (From the Roman perspective.)
- Luke (From the Greek perspective.)
- John (From the Savior's perspective.)

<u>The one book of History:</u>
- Acts (The history of the early church. Could be called the second half of the book of Luke.)

<u>The Pauline (written by Paul) epistles (letters):</u>
- Romans (Written to the church at Rome. The "Constitution of the Christian Church.")
- 1 Corinthians (Written to the church at Corinth. Practical Theology.)
- 2 Corinthians (Information and Instruction to the Corinthian Church.)
- Galatians (Written to the church at Galatia. Justification is by Grace, not Law.)
- Ephesians (Written to the church at Ephesus. Explanation of relationships and roles.)
- Philippians (Written to the church at Philippi. Joy in the Christian walk.)
- Colossians (Written to the church at Colossae. Salvation is through Christ alone.)
- 1 Thessalonians (Written to the church at Thessalonica. Correct doctrine and instruction to the church.)
- 2 Thessalonians (Written to the church at Thessalonica. More of the same.)
- 1 Timothy (Written to his apprentice Timothy. The Leadership manual for the Church.)
- 2 Timothy (Written to his apprentice Timothy. Paul's final words and instructions to Timothy.)
- Titus (Written to his friend Titus. Much the same theme as in Timothy.)
- Philemon (Written to his friend Philemon about a runaway slave who had come to Christ.)

- Hebrews (We don't know for sure who wrote this book. Some attribute it to Paul. Others to Apollos, or other ministers of the time. It was written to Hebrews still in Jerusalem.)

The non-Pauline epistles (named after the authors):
- James (Practical application of the Gospel.)
- 1 Peter (To persecuted Christians.)
- 2 Peter (An exhortation to continue growing in God.)
- 1 John (Strengthening believers and refuting heretics.)
- 2 John ("Stay the course.")
- 3 John (Commendation to Gaius and Condemnation to Diotrephes.)
- Jude (Encouragement to remain doctrinally pure.)

One book of Prophecy (Written by Jesus' disciple John):
- Revelation (Foretelling the destruction of Jerusalem and the ending of the Jewish nation.)

Fun Facts
- The longest book of the Bible is Psalms-150 chapters.
- The shortest book of the Bible is 2 John with one chapter, 13 verses.
- The longest chapter of the Bible is Psalms 119 with 150 verses.
- The shortest chapter of the Bible is Psalms 117 with 2 verses. This is also the middle chapter of the Bible.
- The middle verse of the Bible is Psalms 118:8.
- The shortest verse in the Bible is John 11:35-"Jesus wept."
- The longest verse is Ester 8:9 containing 90 words.
- The Bible Contains:
    3,566,480 letters
    773,693 words
    31,102 verses
    1,189 chapters: 250 in the new, and 939 in the old
- The word "and" appears 46,277 times.
- Reverend appears once.
- "Lord" appears 1,855 times.
- The longest word is: Mahershalalhashbaz. It is found in Isaiah 8:1 and has 18 letters (It is a name).
- The 21st verse of Ezra 7 contains all the letters of the alphabet except J.
- Ester has no mention God.
- Verses 8, 15, 21, and 31 of Psalms 107 are alike.
- Every verse in Psalms 136 ends the same.
- The 19th chapter of 2 Kings and Isaiah 37 are almost identical.

11. Facts About the Bible

- There are about 200 direct quotes in the New Testament from the Old Testament.
- God used forty different men to write the Bible.
- It took at least 1600 years to write the Bible.
- The first Bible printed on a printing press was the Gutenberg Bible, printed in the 1450's
- The first Bible printed is this country was in 1663 in an Indian language.
- There were 25,000,000 Bibles sold in America in 2005, twice the number of Harry Potters from the same year (and this doesn't count digital Bibles available on the internet or phone apps). 100,000,000 were sold worldwide.
- 91% of American Households own a Bible and the average is four per house (meaning most of the Bibles sold each year are to people who already own at least one!).
- 47% of Americans read their Bible at least weekly.
- The Bible has been published in over 450 languages.
- The New Testament alone has been published in nearly 1,400 languages, with the Gospel of Mark in over 2,370 languages.
- This means 90% of the world's population has the Bible available in a language they speak.

12. Which Bible to Use

The King James is the closest to the original of all the most commonly available translations. However, there are no differences between the translations that would make the difference between heaven and hell.

The King James Bible is the simplest, to read. It only has about 8,000 different words as opposed to the NIV, which has over 14,000 different words.

In comparisons of different translations for grade level placement, one scholar came to the following assessment:
- The King James averages grade level- 5.8 (fifth grade, eighth month)
- New International Version- 8.4
- New American Standard Bible- 6.1
- The English Version-7.2
- New KJV- 6.9

A comparison of words in the KJV and the NASB: [3]

	King James	**New American Standard**
Matt1:11	Carried away	Deportation
Luke5:29	Sat	Recline at the table
Matt5:21	Kill	Murder
Matt5:19	Break	Annuls
Luke11:33	Bushel	Peck-measure
Mark5:25	Issue of blood	Hemorrhage
Matt9:18	Certain ruler	Synagogue official
Matt9:17	Bottles	Wineskins
Matt9:13	Mercy	Compassion
Matt8:32	Go	Be gone

I am convinced the KJV is the most accurate English Bible commonly available. It does have some problems, but it came from superior transcripts and had more scholarly translators who actually believed the

---

[3] For more see http://www.av1611.org/kjv/kjveasy.html

Bible was true. Some other translation's translators didn't really believe the Bible was true, especially concerning Creation, before they started and this has affected how they translated certain passages.

There are people that have learned Greek and Hebrew to aid in their study of the Bible. They say that there is nothing like reading It in the original to get the full meaning, but the KJV comes closer than any of the other translations.

It also is written in the most beautiful form the English language has ever taken; Shakespearian English. Not only is God's Word worthy of being presented in the most beautiful form available, this near-poetic language is easier to memorize. See which sticks in the brain better;

- **"First this: God created the Heavens and Earth--all you see, all you don't see. Earth was a soup of nothingness, a bottomless emptiness, an inky blackness. God's Spirit brooded like a bird above the watery abyss."** (The Message Bible)
  or
- **"In the beginning God created the heavens and the earth. And the earth was without form and void and darkness was upon the face of the deep."** (King James Version)

Though similar, the later has a poetic cadence that makes it easier to memorize.

The unfamiliar words (form, void, etc) give me a perfect opportunity to increase my vocabulary. And since the new words are used in real life, I will remember them far better than if they had come from an abstract workbook page.

I will use other translations occasionally as study tools, to get a different perspective on a verse and help me with my understanding, but when there is a difference of translation, I will go with the KJV.

- Psalms 12:6-7 **"The words of the LORD are pure __ __ __ __ __: as __ __ __ __ __ __ tried in a furnace of earth, purified seven times. Thou shalt keep them (His Words), O LORD, thou shalt preserve them from this generation for ever."**

> Matthew 24:35 **"Heaven and earth shall pass away, but My _ _ _ _ _ shall not pass away"**.

"Cling to the whole Bible, not a part of it. A man cannot do much with a broken sword."

The "thee's and thou's" that bother so many in the KJV have a specific purpose. When the King James was translated, thee, thou, thy, and thine were singular pronouns while "you" was plural. (In modern English "you" is both singular and plural, occasionally causing some confusion.) This makes it much clearer who the author is talking to or about.

There are some problems with the KJV, however. For one, the men who translated it added a few verses in, originally as footnotes, that have since been incorporated into the main text. 1 John 5:7 is one of those. This is due to the influence of the very inaccurate Latin Vulgate.

13. Bible Helps

The Concordance

A concordance is an assemblage of every word in the Bible in alphabetical order with all of its locations. The Strong's concordance also links me to the original Hebrew or Greek word and gives the definition of that word. This better allows me to know what the author really meant when he wrote that scripture.

Let's say I want to know where the verse **"For God so loved the world that He gave His only begotten son, that whosoever believeth in Him shall not perish but shall have ever lasting life"** is found.

First I will pick a word to look up- "world."

In the alphabetical listing we find that the word "world" is listed 249 times. This means that in 249 verses, the translators translated a Greek or Hebrew word to "world." Forty-six of these are in the Old Testament. In the 203 New Testament occurrences, three different Greek words (represented by three different numbers; 165, 2889, and 3625) were translated into the word "world." By reading the part of each verse listed we find that the one we want is John 3:16. "World" in this verse is number 2889. We turn to the Greek Lexicon in the back and find that this "world" is κόσμος or in the English alphabet; kosmos. It means:

1) An apt and harmonious arrangement or constitution, order, government.
2) Ornament, decoration, adornment, i.e. the arrangement of the stars, 'the heavenly hosts', as the ornament of the heavens. (1 Peter 3:3)
    a) The world, the universe
    b) The circle of the earth, the earth
3) The inhabitants of the earth, men, the human family
4) The ungodly multitude; the whole mass of men alienated from God, and therefore hostile to the cause of Christ
5) World affairs, the aggregate of things earthly
    a) The whole circle of earthly goods, endowments riches, advantages, pleasures, etc, which although hollow and frail and fleeting, stir desire, seduce from God and are obstacles to the cause of Christ
6) Any aggregate or general collection of particulars of any sort.

a) The Gentiles as contrasted to the Jews (Rom. 11:12 etc)
b) Of believers only, John 1:29; 3:16; 3:17; 6:33; 12:47 1 Corinthians 4:9; 2 Corinthians 5:19

The Strong's is for the King James Bible. There are concordances for other translations also.

Thompson Chain Reference Bible
This is the Bible required by many Bible colleges.

Down the sides of each page are two columns with numbers and scripture "addresses". The addresses take you to other scriptures on the same subject as the adjoining verses. The numbers take you to a supplement in the back that lists scriptures by subjects. Before this supplement is a Table of Contents that lists all the different subjects so you can look up whichever one you need.

The Thompson Chain also has a concordance (not as complete as Strong's, of course), maps, charts about the life of Christ and other prominent Bible characters, summaries of each book in the Bible, and an archeological supplement.

Center Reference
(Cambridge is one brand) These Bibles have a column down the middle of the page with small numbers or letters followed by definitions of words in the corresponding scripture and sometimes other verses on the same subjects.

Bible Dictionary
This is a dictionary specific to giving you the Biblical definitions of words and terms. Vines and Ungers are good. For a good none-biblical dictionary try the Webster's Original 1828 dictionary (available on line, from Amazon and from a number of booksellers).

Comparative Bible
This is a Bible that has more than one translation in the same book. It will have one translation in one column and another right next to that. These are good for Bible studies. They have from two to twelve different versions in one book.

Interlinear Bibles
These are Greek or Hebrew Bibles with the direct English translation written underneath each word.

Bible Atlas
This is a book of maps, pictures and information about the biblical region of the world (modern day Palestine). They usually have different maps of the same area marked for different time periods. For example, one map may be marked for the travels of Moses and the next for Joshua's travels, while a later one is marked for the travels of Christ and another for Paul's journeys.

Bible Commentary
A book (usually containing the Bible itself) that contains comments written to explain the scripture. For example:

(Scripture) Genesis 1:1 In the beginning God created the heavens and the earth.

(Commentary) "The word "God" here is "Elohim" which means "God" in the majestic plural tense (This is the tense royalty uses to refer to themselves. It does not mean more than one as our plural does, but a plurality of greatness.) It is using a singular verb.

"This could be worded: "In the beginning of time, God made space and matter," though it wouldn't be as poetic.

"Psalms 90:2 says 'Before the mountains were brought forth, or ever thou hadst formed the earth and the world, even from everlasting to everlasting, thou art God.'

"Some put a gap of several million years here. Is this correct interpretation of the Bible?

"First of all, who wrote this? The traditionally accepted author is Moses, though some believe he only compiled several books written by many previous authors. These people believe Adam himself may have written down this scripture as God dictated it to him. Either way, the purpose of this scripture was to tell all those following the author in history how the earth began. Does it make since for there to be a gap of millions of years here that is not mentioned at all? Would that fulfill its purpose?

"The entire idea of 'the gap' is to allow for evolution and explain the fossil record. Millions of years of evolution, dinosaurs, and many other creatures were to have lived and died between verse one and verse two..."[4]

Important!

Remember that commentaries and all these helps, as well as the Internet, are written by human beings. They are fallible. They may help me understand the Bible or they may confuse me, or even lead me into lies. I will use them carefully and always check EVERYTHING out with the Bible itself.

EVERY Christian should read the entire Bible, cover to cover, at least three times and frequently thereafter (Our pastor challenges us to read through it every other year) before reading any commentaries. This applies to the Internet also. This may even be true for listening to preachers on the radio who are not my pastor. It is important to be well founded in what really is in the Bible before I listen to humans.

Online Resources

You can find the entire Bible in several translations many places, including:
http://www.biblegateway.com/
http://www.blueletterbible.org/
http://BibleHub.com/.

The Blue Letter Bible and BibleHub also contains Strong's concordance linked to each word. Bible Gateway includes many translations (among them, interlinear Bibles), while BibleHub will compare verses from fifteen different translations at once. BibleHub also has maps and dictionaries.

Matthew Henry was a scholar who lived in the 1800's and wrote a detailed commentary on the entire Bible. It is very complete and informative. It is one commentary available at both BlueLetter and

---

[4] From "First Things First: The Book of Genesis" by Betty Tracy

BibleHub.

    Youtube.com has many preachers available who I can learn a great deal from. However, I will keep in mind they are human and can be mistaken. I will <u>ALWAYS</u> check out what they say with my Bible and my pastor.

14. Church Attendance

Becoming part of a local church is an important step in my Christian walk.

Conditions of church attendance

Attending a church will not take the place of being born again, but since I have accepted Christ as my savior, I am ready to commit to a local church.

➢ Romans 10:13 "For _____ shall call upon the name of the Lord shall be _____."

➢ Acts 16:31 "And they said, _____ on the Lord Jesus Christ and thou shalt be _____, and thy house."

➢ Acts 2:47 "…And the Lord _____ to the church daily such as should be _____."

Why should I attend church?

The word "church" in the Greek New Testament means "assembly" or group of believers meeting together. (Acts 4:31)

- To worship God. He deserves my praise in every way I can give it- alone and with other believers.

- The disciples set the pattern. Acts 2:42 "**And they _____ steadfastly in the apostles' doctrine and fellowship, and in** _____ **of bread, and in prayers.**"

- Strength comes from unity. I need a church to serve in; and, other believers need my testimony for Christ.

- I cannot be a well-rounded, healthy Christian outside of the church. We keep each other balanced.

- I need the fellowship of God's people and the united prayers of fellow believers.

- Christ's command of Matthew 28:19, 20 applies as much to me today as to those of His time.

"Go ye therefore, and __ __ __ __ __ all nations, baptizing them in the name of the Father, and of the Son, and of the Holy Ghost: __ __ __ __ __ __ __ __ them to observe all things whatsoever I have commanded you: and, lo, I am with you alway, even unto the end of the world. Amen."

Attending church prepares and strengthens me to do this.

- The church provides opportunity for me to witness and serve.

➢ 1 Corinthians 3:9 **"For we are __ __ __ __ __ __ __ __ together with God: ye are God's husbandry, ye are God's building."**

- God commanded submission to the leadership in a church. I can't fulfill that command unless I actually belong to a church.

- I have more mature Christians to teach me about God.

- I belong.

When should I become active in a local church?

As soon as I'm born again into God's family.

➢ 1 Corinthians 12:27 **"Now ye are the __ __ __ __ of Christ, and __ __ __ __ __ __ __ in particular."**

The entire church is compared to a body of which Christ is the true head and the believers are members (limbs, etc). As a member of the body of Christ, I want to function and find my place of service.

➢ Colossians 1:18 **"And He is the head of the __ __ __ __, the __ __ __ __ __ __."**

➢ Matthew 16:16 **"... Peter said, 'Thou art the __ __ __ __ __ __, the Son of the Living God.'"**

14. Church Attendance

If this also is my true confession of Christ, then I should identify with my fellow believers in a local church.

What are my responsibilities to my church?

- My love and faithfulness. Hebrews 10:25 **"Not forsaking the __ __ __ __ __ __ __ __ __ __ of ourselves together, as the manner of some is; but __ __ __ __ __ __ __ __ __ one another: and so much the more, as ye see the day approaching."**

- Maintain regular attendance; be dependable.

- Give to support its programs (churches have mortgages, electric bills, gas bills, etc. just like businesses and households do.)

- Keeping its teachings.

- Testifying: 2 Timothy 1:8 **"Be not thou therefore __ __ __ __ __ __ __ __ of the testimony of our Lord, nor of me his prisoner: but be thou __ __ __ __ __ __ __ __ of the afflictions of the gospel according to the power of God;"**

- Witnessing. Luke 8:39 **"Return to thine own house, and __ __ __ __ how great things God hath __ __ __ __ unto thee…"**

- Serving. 1 Thessalonians 1:3 **"…remembering without ceasing your __ __ __ __ of faith, and __ __ __ __ __ of love, and patience of hope in our Lord Jesus Christ, in the sight of God and our father;"**

- Loving the brethren John 13:35 **"By this shall all men __ __ __ __ that yea are my disciples, if ye have __ __ __ __ for one another."**

Can I claim to love God but not wish to be bound to one church any more than I can love someone but refuse to marry because of the responsibilities?

Can I claim to be a good Christian and not serve in my local church any more than I can be a good citizen of my country and enjoy its privileges but refuse to pay taxes, vote, or fight for my freedoms?

Can I claim to love my brothers, especially those in leadership, and not be there to support them and allow them to teach me?

14. Church Attendance

- James 3:1 "**My brethren, be not many masters** (teachers, preachers, pastors,) **knowing that we shall receive the greater** __ __ __ __ __ __ __ __ __ __ __ __."
- Hebrews 13:17 "__ __ __ __ **them that have the rule over you, and** __ __ __ __ __ __ **yourselves: for they watch for you** __ __ __ __ __, **as they that must give** __ __ __ __ __ __ __ , **that they may do it with** __ __ __, **and not with** __ __ __ __ __: **for that is unprofitable for** __ __ __."

The leaders in a church will be held accountable for my salvation and strength in God. I won't make their job impossible by not actually being there for the spiritual meal they prepare for me every week.

- Acts 20:28 "**Take heed therefore unto yourselves, and to all the** __ __ __ __ __, **over the which the Holy Ghost hath made you** __ __ __ __ __ __ __ __ __, **to feed the church of God…**"

How often should I go to church?
- Hebrews 13:17 "__ __ __ __ them that have the rule over you, and __ __ __ __ __ __ yourselves: for they watch for your __ __ __ __ __ __, as they that must give account, that they may do it with joy, and not with __ __ __ __ __: for that is unprofitable for you."

Different groups at different times and places throughout the church age have required their people to attend services on different schedules. Sometimes meetings were held once a month. Sometimes several times a week. Today, some Amish groups meet every other week. Some fundamentalist churches meet four times a week.

God put specific men in charge of my church to watch out for my soul. Those men pray and decide what schedule best fit the needs of me and the other members of my congregation.

In the American culture this usually means a worship service on Sunday morning and a Bible study later in the week. The worship service allows me to give God glory with my brothers and sisters in the Lord and to gain from preaching and fellowship. The Bible study allows a time for me to be taught more intensely and to ask questions, getting more personal direction for my life. Both are necessary.

I also need a time each week for service to the Body of Christ. My church may have special programs or groups to facilitate this, or they may have ideas to help me find my personal calling. I need to ask.

Suggestions for meaningful worship
> John 4:24 **"God is a __ __ __ __ __ __: and they that worship Him must worship Him in __ __ __ __ __ __ and in __ __ __ __ __."**

I will...
- Bow my head for silent prayer prior to service.
- Pray for my minister, for those serving, and for each other and for myself on a regular basis.
- Pray that God's Word will find lodging in the hearts and lives of the congregation and community.
- Sing the hymns. Meditate on the song message as I worship.
- Use my Bible. Turn to the scriptures used. Underline the portions expounded and made meaningful in the sermon.
- Take notes on the sermon and apply the teaching to my daily life.
- Avoid talking, laughing and whispering during the service. (except where appropriate; it's ok to laugh if the preacher tells a joke.)
- After the service, fellowship with those in attendance.

My attitude towards God's house
I should...

- Respect and love it.
- Defend the church against scoffers and unbelievers.
- Be mindful of the church appearance and atmosphere. I will do what I can to improve and maintain it. Someone needs to scrub the toilets, vacuum the floor, and pull the weeds. Why not me?
- Contribute to the upkeep of God's house in both time and money.
- Cooperate.

The church is not just a building. The church is an assembled body of believers. We are the temple of the living God.

➢ 1 Corinthians 3:16, 17 **"Know ye not that ye are the __ __ __ __ __ __ of God and that the spirit of God __ __ __ __ __ __ __ __ in you? If any man __ __ __ __ __ __ the temple of God, him shall God destroy; for the temple of God is __ __ __ __, which temple ye are."**

My absence...

- Aids the devil in overcoming souls.
- Weakens my spiritual life.
- Makes a poor witness to others.
- Causes Christianity to be questioned.
- Makes me vulnerable to the world.
- Makes the minister's job more difficult. It is hard to prepare a meal when you never know how many will be there to eat. It is discouraging to prepare a twelve-course meal and have no one show up. Yet it is the minister's responsibility to make sure I learn the things I need to. This is impossible to do if I am not there.
- Weakens the fellowship.
- Discourages the brothers.

When I am not there, my chair screams "Empty."

The Importance Of Choosing The Right Church

I need to choose a church that is Bible centered; I know that what is taught at the church I attend helps to shape my new life in Christ. The type of Christian I will be in a few years will depend greatly on the church that I attend regularly. A few of the ways in which the church helps to shape my life:

- My church determines what I am taught or not taught about the Bible.
- My church provides avenues of spiritual growth and fellowship.
- My church is the launching pad for my service for God.
- My church encourages me to do soul winning.
- My church trains me in Christian living.
- My church furnishes me with prayer warriors- people who will stand with me during times of sickness, death, and adversity.
- My church gives me a missionary vision.

- My church influences what my children will believe about spiritual matters.
- My church influences my depth of spiritual maturity. It can cause me to be a shallow, ineffective Christian; or, it can help me become a deeply spiritual Christian.

I will choose my church carefully.

If necessary, it is better to travel a little distance to attend a Bible centered church than to go to a church that is doctrinally unsound close by.

If I am careful about selecting the clothes I wear, the food I eat and the place in which I live, I should be even more careful about the church I attend.

The church in which I accepted Christ would more than likely be a good place for me to attend as there would be a special interest in me as a new convert. However, God often moves people to a new church after a few years to teach them more about Him.

Above all, pray about this most serious decision.

15. Water Baptism
Meaning and Importance

Water Baptism is an outward sign of an inward work. It gives testimony of a changed life.

Why is it Important?

Jesus was baptized of John to fulfill scripture and left us an example to follow.

➢ Matthew 3:15b **"Suffer it to be so now: for thus it becometh us to _ _ _ _ _ _ _ all _ _ _ _ _ _ _ _ _ _ _ _ _ _ _ _."**

I have the example of the disciples.

➢ Acts 19:5 **"When they heard this, they were _ _ _ _ _ _ _ _ the name of the Lord Jesus."**

I have the promise of the gift of the Holy Ghost.

➢ Acts 2:38b **"_ _ _ _ _ _ and be _ _ _ _ _ _ _ _ everyone of you in the name of Jesus Christ for (because of) the remission of _ _ _ _, and ye shall receive the gift of the Holy Ghost."**

It is an act of my obedience

➢ John 14:15 **"If ye _ _ _ _ me, keep my _ _ _ _ _ _ _ _ _ _ _."**

I am now a follower of Christ. It is my privilege to follow the Lord in being baptized in water.

➢ Mark 16:16 **"He that _ _ _ _ _ _ _ _ _ and is _ _ _ _ _ _ _ _ shall be saved; but he that believeth not shall be _ _ _ _ _ _."**

What is the significance?

➢ Romans 6:4 "Therefore we are __ __ __ __ __ __ with Him by baptism into __ __ __ __ __ that like as Christ was raised up from the dead by the glory of the Father, even so we also should __ __ __ __ in newness of life."

It is a testimony of my love and obedience to the Lord before my unsaved friends, family and to my fellow believers.

Mode or Method of Baptism

"Baptize" means "to dip or immerse, to be covered by water, put completely under, buried."

➢ Colossians 2:12 "Buried with Him in __ __ __ __ __ __ __, wherein also ye are __ __ __ __ __ with Him through the __ __ __ __ __ of the operation of God, who hath raised Him from the dead."

Immersion in water (baptism) typifies the death, burial and resurrection of our Lord. I go completely under the waters of baptism (for just a second); an act on my part to symbolically bury my old life (death to self) and come up in newness of life in Christ.

After I have given my life to God, I will meet with my pastor to discuss being baptized. A date will be set so I can invite any family or friends I want to be there.

I will need to bring a dry change of clothes and a couple of towels.

16. The Gift of the Holy Ghost

The promise to the believer "is unto you and to your children and to all that are afar off, even as many as the Lord our God shall call" Acts 2:38

Introduction

Before the birth and life of Jesus the Holy Ghost was promised through prophecy.

- Joel 2:28-29 "And it shall come to pass afterward, that I will pour out My __ __ __ __ __ __ upon all flesh, and your sons and your daughters shall __ __ __ __ __ __ __ __, your old men shall dream __ __ __ __ __ __, your young men shall see __ __ __ __ __ __ __. And also upon the servants and upon the handmaids in those days will I pour out my __ __ __ __ __ __."

The Holy Ghost is a promise

It is a gift from God and is promised to all who believe.

- Acts 2:38-39 "Then Peter said unto them, '__ __ __ __ __ __ and be __ __ __ __ __ __ __ __ every one of you in the name of Jesus Christ for the remission of __ __ __ __, and ye shall receive the gift of the __ __ __ __ __ __ __ __ __. For the __ __ __ __ __ __ __ is unto you and to your children and to __ __ __ that are afar off, even as many as the Lord our God shall call.'"

Who is the Holy Ghost?

Jesus said:

- John 14:16 "And I will pray the Father and He shall give you another __ __ __ __ __ __ __ __ __, that He may abide with you forever; even the __ __ __ __ __ __ of truth; …but ye know Him (present tense; this is before Christ's crucifixion) **for He dwelleth with you (present tense), and shall be in you. __ will not leave you comfortless: __ __ __ __ __ COME TO YOU.**"

Jesus promised to come to me as the Comforter.

16. The Gift of the Holy Ghost

➤ John 14:26 **"But the Comforter which is the __ __ __ __ __ __ __ __ __ whom the Father will send in my name, He shall teach you all things."**

If I have repented of my sins and accepted Jesus into my heart, I am a child of God and in a saved condition. However God has promised something more for me. Now I need the Gift of the Holy Ghost for many purposes.

- Comfort: John 14:18 **"I will not leave you __ __ __ __ __ __ __ __ __ __ __. I will come to you."**

- Teacher, Revealer: John 14:26 **"But the __ __ __ __ __ __ __ __ __ __, which is the Holy Ghost, whom the Father will send in My Name, He shall __ __ __ __ __ you all things and bring all things to your __ __ __ __ __ __ __ __ __ __ whatsoever I have said unto you."**

- Guidance: John 16:13 **"Howbeit when He, the Spirit of __ __ __ __ __, is come He will __ __ __ __ __ you into all truth."**

- Power: Acts 1:8 **"But ye shall receive __ __ __ __ __ after that the Holy Ghost is __ __ __ __ upon you."**

Gifts of the Holy Ghost

There are nine Gifts of The Spirit. These gifts are found in 1 Corinthians 12:8-10.

➤ **"For to one is given by The Spirit the word of __ __ __ __ __ __
To another the word of __ __ __ __ __ __ __ __ __ by the same Spirit;
To another __ __ __ __ __ by the same Spirit;
To another the gifts of __ __ __ __ __ __ __ by the same Spirit;
To another the working of __ __ __ __ __ __ __ __,
To another prophecy,
To another __ __ __ __ __ __ __ __ __ __ of spirits,
To another divers kinds of __ __ __ __ __ __ __;
To another the __ __ __ __ __ __ __ __ __ __ __ __ of tongues."**

God will call upon me for the use of these gifts, as they are needed in

16. The Gift of the Holy Ghost

His service.

How do I know if I have the Holy Ghost?
There are many examples of people receiving the Holy Ghost in the scripture.

One example is Acts 2:4 **"And they were all _ _ _ _ _ _ with the Holy Ghost and began to _ _ _ _ _ with other _ _ _ _ _ _ _ as the Spirit gave them utterance."**

- Acts 10:45-46 **"And they of the circumcision which _ _ _ _ _ _ _ were astonished, as many as came with Peter, because that on the Gentiles also was poured out the _ _ _ _ of the Holy Ghost. For they heard them _ _ _ _ _ with tongues and _ _ _ _ _ _ God."**

- Acts 19:6 **"And when Paul had laid his _ _ _ _ _ upon them, the Holy _ _ _ _ _ came on them and they spake with Tongues and _ _ _ _ _ _ _ _ _ _."**

- Isaiah 28:11 **"For with _ _ _ _ _ _ _ _ _ _ lips and another tongue will he _ _ _ _ _ to this people."**

Someone "Speaks in Tongues" when they yield control of their mouth to God. They are fully conscious and otherwise in full control of themselves. Their spirit is praying to God about things their conscious mind can't put into words.

The Bible does not say that speaking in tongues is the only evidence of the Holy Ghost. Someone who exhibits another Fruit of the Spirit (such as prophecy or healing) definitely has the Holy Ghost even if they haven't spoken in tongues.

Receiving the Holy Ghost:
I will look to the Word of God for examples of how people in the early church received the Holy Ghost.

- Acts 2:1-4 **"And when the day of Pentecost was fully come, they**

16. The Gift of the Holy Ghost

were all with __ __ __ accord in one place.

v2 And suddenly there came a sound from heaven as of a rushing mighty __ __ __ __, and it filled all the house where they were sitting,

v3 and there appeared unto them cloven __ __ __ __ __ __ like as of fire, and it sat upon each of them.

v4 And they were all filled with the __ __ __ __ __ __ __ __ __ and began to __ __ __ __ __ with other tongues as the __ __ __ __ __ __ gave them utterance."

This is the first record of people receiving the Gift of the Holy Ghost. These people were probably worshipping God when they received this brand new experience. I'll look at another example of people receiving the gift of the Holy Ghost.

➢ Acts 8:17 **"Then __ __ __ __ they their hands on them and they __ __ __ __ __ __ __ __ the Holy Ghost."**

➢ Acts 19:6 **"And when Paul had laid his __ __ __ __ __ upon them, the __ __ __ __ __ __ __ __ __ came on them and they spake with tongues and __ __ __ __ __ __ __ __ __."**

I see examples of God's people receiving the Holy Ghost when praying and worshipping God. I also have examples of them being filled when the Apostles laid hands on them. Many people receive the Holy Ghost in many different ways. But this I know, that Jesus said …

➢ Luke 24:49 **"And behold I send the __ __ __ __ __ __ __ of my Father upon you: but __ __ __ __ __ ye in the city of Jerusalem, until ye be endued with __ __ __ __ __ from on high."**

The word tarry means to wait, so I should not be satisfied until I am filled with God's Spirit. I should spend time in prayer, worshipping and thanking God for His goodness to me. I should yield my being to Him.

I have a promise from Jesus that if I …

16. The Gift of the Holy Ghost

➤ Luke 11:9 "… ask and it shall be __ __ __ __ __ you: seek and ye shall __ __ __ __, knock, and it shall be __ __ __ __ __ __ unto you."

I won't live beneath my privilege. God wants me to receive this Wonderful Gift.

➤ 1 Corinthians 5:8 "Therefore let us keep the __ __ __ __ __, not with old leaven, neither with the __ __ __ __ __ __ of malice and wickedness; but with the unleavened __ __ __ __ __ of sincerity and truth."

17. Home Worship, Family Alter and Quiet Time

Family Alter; a time of united blessings, and a sharing together of spiritual growth.

Family Alter Time is worshipping God in the home.

➢ Joshua 24:15 "...as for me and my _ _ _ _ _, we will serve the Lord."

My children are not my own, but special gifts from God. It is my responsibility to raise them to love Him.

My children and I need God's teaching just as Mary, who

➢ Luke 10:39 "...sat Jesus' feet, and _ _ _ _ _ his word."

Job offered sacrifices for each of his children.

➢ Job 1:5 "And it was so, when the days of their feasting were gone about, that Job sent and _ _ _ _ _ _ _ _ _ _ them, and rose up early in the morning, and offered burnt _ _ _ _ _ _ _ _ _ according to the number of them all:"

I do not offer sacrifices for my children. However, as a parent, I need to pray with and for my children.

I need to be concerned about my family coming to Christ just as was Andrew, who led his brother Simon Peter to Christ.

➢ John 1:41 "He first findeth his own _ _ _ _ _ _ _ Simon and saith unto him, we have found the _ _ _ _ _ _ _."

I need to pray for the conversion of my entire household.

➢ Acts 16:15 "And when she was baptized, and her _ _ _ _ _ _ _ _ _..."

➢ Acts 16:25-34 relates the conversion and baptisms of the Philippian

17. Home Worship, Family Alter and Quiet Time

jailer and his family: **"And at midnight Paul and Silas** __ __ __ __ __ __, **and** __ __ __ __ **praises unto God: and the prisoners heard them.**

v26 And suddenly there was a great earthquake, so that the foundations of the prison were shaken: and immediately all the doors were opened, and every one's __ __ __ __ __ were loosed.

v27 And the keeper of the prison awaking out of his sleep, and seeing the prison doors __ __ __ __, he drew out his sword, and would have __ __ __ __ __ __ himself, supposing that the prisoners had been fled.

v28 But Paul cried with a loud voice, saying, 'Do thyself no harm: for we are __ __ __ here.'

v29 Then he called for a light, and sprang in, and came trembling, and fell down before Paul and Silas,

v30 And brought them out, and said, 'Sirs, what must I do to be __ __ __ __ __?'

v31 And they said, '__ __ __ __ __ __ __ on the Lord Jesus Christ, and thou shalt be saved, and thy __ __ __ __ __.'

v32 And they spake unto him the word of the Lord, and to __ __ __ that were in his house.

v33 And he took them the same hour of the night, and washed their stripes; and was __ __ __ __ __ __ __ __, he and __ __ __ his, straightway.

v34 And when he had brought them into his house, he set meat before them, and rejoiced, believing in God with __ __ __ his __ __ __ __ __."

Since God gave me every minute of my life in the first place, it is worth the effort to find time to give back to Him daily.

Why do I need a Family Alter Time?

17. Home Worship, Family Alter and Quiet Time

- It builds spiritual stature and depth in all members of the family.
- The Family Alter Time aids Bible learning for the whole family.
- Training is secured through the Family Alter Time. This is where mighty warriors for Christ get their training. The children in my home today will become the warriors in the Kingdom of God tomorrow. This is the time to teach them to use their Sword- the Word of God.
- The Family Alter Time stimulates family unity. It sweetens the family life of every Christian, builds memories, and enriches the home.
- Prayer life is furthered here.
- The Family Alter Time will help dissolve the misunderstandings that occur whenever you have humans living together, and will relieve friction. Romans 12:9-11 **"Let love be without _ _ _ _ _ _ _ _ _ _ _ _ _. Abhor that which is evil; cleave to that which is _ _ _ _.**
Be _ _ _ _ _ _ _ affectioned one to another with _ _ _ _ _ _ _ _ _ love; in honor _ _ _ _ _ _ _ _ _ _ one another;

Not slothful in business; fervent in spirit; serving the Lord;"

- It is a way to influence any guest I may have in my home.

Romans 14:7 **"For none of us _ _ _ _ _ _ to himself, and no man dieth to himself."**

- My Family Alter Time will become a foundation stone to my church. No church is any stronger than the families that make it up. Romans 6:17 **"But God be thanked, that ye were the servants of _ _ _, but ye have _ _ _ _ _ _ from the heart that form of doctrine which was delivered you."**

- I will become an example to other families of what is possible to achieve for God and what a good Christian family looks like. Acts 2:46,47 **"And they, continuing _ _ _ _ _ with one accord in the temple, and breaking _ _ _ _ _ from house to house, did eat their meat with _ _ _ _ _ _ _ and singleness of heart,"**

- The Bible requires the Family Alter time. We are always blessed when we obey. Deuteronomy 6:7 **"And thou shalt _ _ _ _ _ [My Words] diligently unto thy _ _ _ _ _ _ _ _..."**

17. Home Worship, Family Alter and Quiet Time

Ephesians 6:4 "And ye __ __ __ __ __ __ __, don't frustrate your __ __ __ __ __ __ __ __, but bring them up in the culture and education of the __ __ __ __." (Paraphrase)

I will find a place and time for Family Alter Time

- I will find a quiet area for my family worship. It may be around a table, a piano, in the living room, bedroom, maybe the den.

- I will set a definite 15-20 minutes aside each day. This time should be free of interference and convenient for all family members. I should look at my family's current schedule and find a daily event (such as eating breakfast or going to bed) that I can attach our Family Alter time to in order to make it easier to form the habit of doing it.

- Radios, televisions, MP3 players, video games, computers, telephones or any other elements that would distract attention MUST be turned off.

- Someone should take the lead. The family should plan together with one person directing. Usually the Christian father is the leader. This Bible precedent was set by many in the Word. Among the men who were spiritual leaders of their households were:

  o Abraham: Genesis 18:19 **"For I __ __ __ __ him, that he will command his children and his household after him, and they shall __ __ __ __ the way of the Lord, to do justice and judgment ; that the Lord may bring upon Abraham that which He hath spoken of him."**

  o Jacob: Genesis 35:2 **"Then Jacob said unto his household, and to all that were with him, 'Put __ __ __ __ the strange gods that are among you, and be __ __ __ __ __, and change your garments.'"**

  o Isaac blessed his son: Genesis 27:26-27 **"And his father Isaac said unto him, Come near now, and kiss me, my son.**

    v27 **And he came near, and kissed him: and he smelled the smell of his raiment, and blessed him, and said, See, the smell of my son is as the smell of a field which the LORD hath blessed:"**

  o Sampson's father prayed for guidance to rear his son. Judges 13:8, 12 **"Then Manoah entreated the LORD, and said, O my Lord, let the man of God which thou didst send come again unto us, and __ __**

17. Home Worship, Family Alter and Quiet Time

__ __ __ us what we shall ... do unto the child that shall be born. and Manoah said now let thy words come to pass "

- David gave advice to his son Solomon. **1 Kings 2:2-3 "I go the way of all the earth: be thou __ __ __ __ __ __ therefore, and shew thyself a man;**

    v3 And __ __ __ __ the charge of the LORD thy God, to walk in his ways, to keep his __ __ __ __ __ __ __ __, and his commandments, and his __ __ __ __ __ __ __ __, and his testimonies, as it is written in the law of Moses, that thou mayest prosper in all that thou doest, and whithersoever thou turnest thyself:"

- Cornelius headed a religious household. Acts 10:2 **"A devout man, and one that feared God with all his __ __ __ __ __, which gave much alms to the people, and prayed to God always."**

However, if the father does not lead, the mother or another person should accept the position. Every member should participate.

The family that prays together, stays together

Some ideas for Family Alter Time

- If someone comes to the door, I will politely ask them to join us or to return later.

- We will sing hymns for enjoyment and for providing mood. They help everyone get their mind on God. I can find music and words at my church, on the Internet, or at my local Bible Book store.

- We can take turns reading the Scriptures. This increases everyone's skills at reading.

- We can take turns praying. Everyone needs to learn to speak to God.

- We will discuss what we have read. We will ask children questions and let them ask us questions. We could also let them draw a picture representing the day's reading.

- Some enjoy using Bible storybooks or devotionals during Family Alter time. If I use them, I will keep in mind that such helps are written by humans and are not the inspired Word of God. They may be good aids at

17. Home Worship, Family Alter and Quiet Time

first, while I am becoming familiar with the Bible, but they are not necessary as God is capable of speaking to even small children through His Word alone.

- We can share experiences from the day and how God helped or how the Word was applied.

- We can practice Bible memory verses.

- We can discuss family needs and problems applying God's Word for the solution.

Private Devotions

Not only should each member of the family be actively involved in the Family Alter Time, each member should have an individual quiet time with the Lord. This helps us draw even closer to God on a personal basis.

- It will send me into my day with a better attitude, more strength to work for God, and greater determination to use my life to bring glory to God. Colossians 3:17 **"And __ __ __ __ __ __ __ __ __ __ ye do in word or deed, do all in the name of the Lord Jesus, giving __ __ __ __ __ __ to God and the Father by Him."**

- It will give me strength to meet the discouragements, disappointments, unexpected adversities, and sometimes the blind hopes that fall in my path. Hebrews 2:18 **"For in that He Himself hath __ __ __ __ __ __ __ __ being tempted, He is able to succour** (help) **them that are __ __ __ __ __ __ __."**

- It makes me conscious throughout the day of the presence of God who will bring me through more than a conqueror over every unholy thought or thing that rises up against me.

Philippians 4:5-7 **"Let your __ __ __ __ __ __ __ __ __ be known unto all men. The Lord is at hand.**

v6 Be careful for __ __ __ __ __ __ __; but in everything by __ __ __ __ __ __ and supplication with __ __ __ __ __ __ __ __ __ __ __ let your requests be made known unto God.

v7 And the peace of God, which passeth all understanding, shall keep your __ __ __ __ __ __ and __ __ __ __ __ through Christ Jesus."

- It gives me a time to be quiet and hear God speak to me personally or to just bask in His presence.

Simply reading one chapter and praying every morning will greatly increase my closeness to God.

Marital Fellowship with God
It strengthens marriages for a couple to spend time with their Bible and their God. Again, just a chapter and a time of prayer together makes a tremendous difference.

My relationship with God and my spouse is an equilateral triangle. The closer we come to each other, the closer we come to God. The closer we come to God the closer we come to each other. Marital devotion times are ideal for achieving this.

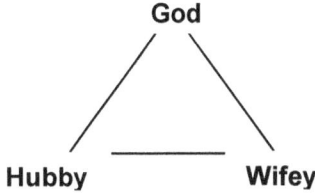

18. Witnessing

➢ Mark 16:15 "**And he said to them, Go you into all the __ __ __ __ __, and preach the gospel to every __ __ __ __ __ __ __ __.**"

➢ Matthew 28:**19 "Go you therefore, and __ __ __ __ __ all nations, baptizing them in the name of the Father, and of the Son, and of the Holy Ghost:"**

Jesus gave these commands to all His followers, not just the ministry. It is the responsibility of every believer to do all they can to bring all they come in contact with to God.

If I love my neighbor as much as I love myself, I don't want them to go to Hell any more than I want to go to Hell myself. I want them to know the joy of serving God and having His forgiveness.

The first way I can witness to those around me is by the life I live.

➢ 1 Thessalonians 5:22 "**Abstain from all __ __ __ __ __ __ __ __ __ __ of __ __ __ __.**"

There are sometimes things that are not sins but appear to others to be sins. For the sake of those who don't know God and those who are younger in God than I am, I will abstain.

➢ 1 Corinthians 8:13 "**Why, if meat make my brother to __ __ __ __ __ __, I will eat no flesh while the world stands, lest I make my brother to offend.**"

There was no sin in eating meat. But to protect his fellow Christians, Paul determined he would not eat meat wherever it caused problems. I should have the same attitude towards my brothers.

➢ John 13:35 "**By this shall all men __ __ __ __ that you are my disciples, if you have __ __ __ __ one to another.**"

Though many religions have an element of love, Christianity is the only one that is based on love. If I choose the loving path every time, I will show the love of God to others. This means I will do all I can to help my fellow Christians in their walk with God, as well as living love to the unsaved in my life.

"Our actions are the only sermon many people will ever hear."

I don't want to beat people over the head or become obnoxious with my faith, but I do want to take every chance possible to tell them about Jesus and the wonderful things He has done in my life.

What do I do if they accept Jesus as their Boss?

If someone I am witnessing to accepts Jesus as their savior, it becomes my responsibility to help them get started on their walk with God. Just like a Mamma sheep nurses, protects and cares for her lambs, I become like a spiritual Mamma to this new baby Christian.

I will need to teach them to read their Bible and pray, and encourage them to commit to a church. I will need to be available to answer questions. I will probably need to arrange to meet them on a weekly basis to answer questions.

If I need guidance, I can go to my pastor or my spiritual "mamma" for help.

19. Tithing and Stewardship

God will be no man's debtor. Man gives to God with a teaspoon;
God gives back to man with a shovel.

What is Tithing?

The word "tithe" means "a tenth;" one tenth of the annual produce of one's land or its equivalent in money.

- In Genesis 14:20 Abraham gave tithes of all he had.

- Jacob promised God a tenth. Genesis 28:22 **"...I will surely give the _ _ _ _ _ unto Thee."**

- Leviticus 27:30 Tells Israel to give a tenth of land, fruit or seed.

- The children of Israel brought tithes of all things. 2 Chronicles 31:5b **"... and the tithe of _ _ _ things brought they in abundantly."**

I will gladly bring a tenth, (or tithe), of my income and possessions.

What is an Offering?

An offering is a gift to God above my tithes.

To Whom Does all My Money and Other Possessions Belong?

➤ 1 Timothy 6:7 **"For we brought _ _ _ _ _ _ _ into this world, and it is certain we can carry nothing _ _ _."**

God gives me the ability and skill to earn my money; so, all I have I owe to God.

➤ Haggai 2:8 **"'The _ _ _ _ _ _ is mine, and the _ _ _ _ is mine,' saith the Lord of hosts."**

➤ Psalms 24:1 **"The _ _ _ _ _ is the Lord's, and the fullness thereof; the _ _ _ _ _, and they that dwell therein."**

Acknowledging that I don't really own anything, but that it all belongs

19. Tithing and Stewardship

to God anyway, makes it easier to give to support His work. It is not difficult to give God $1 back out of every $10 He gives me.

When do I Give Tithes?
➢ 1 Corinthians 16:2 **"Upon the first day of the _ _ _ _ let every one of you lay by him in store, as God hath _ _ _ _ _ _ _ _ _ him…"**

I should set aside a regular time to give so that it becomes a habit. Most people find payday (or the first service afterward) to be the easiest, whether weekly or monthly. I might want to see if my church has a Paypal account to ease my giving even more.[5]

Where do I Bring My Tithe?
➢ Malachi 3:10 **"Bring yea all the _ _ _ _ _ _ into the storehouse that there may be _ _ _ _ in mine house…"**

The storehouse is God's house (the local church I attend) where I receive my spiritual food. The work of the local church is carried on by the tithes and offerings given by God's people.

Some of my tithes and offerings will go to pay my Pastor. Since he feeds me spiritually, it is right for the church to feed him physically.

➢ 1 Corinthians 9:9 **"For it is written in the law of Moses, You shall not _ _ _ _ _ _ the mouth of the _ _ that treads out the corn. Does God take care for oxen?**

v10 Or said he it altogether for our sakes? For our sakes, no doubt, this is written: that he that _ _ _ _ _ should plow in hope; and that he that threshes in hope should be _ _ _ _ _ _ _ _ of his hope.

v11 If we have sown to you _ _ _ _ _ _ _ _ things, is it a great thing if we shall reap your _ _ _ _ _ _ things?"

Some of my gifts to the church will go to pay the mortgage, utilities, buy learning materials, and other expenses of the ministry.

---

[5] Bread of Life's paypal account is at OurChurch@BreadOfLifeCF.com

What Should be My Attitude in My Giving?

➢ 2 Corinthians 9:7 "Every man according as he _____ in his heart so let him give; not _____, or of necessity: for God loveth a _____ giver."

I will purpose to give my tithe. I will set it aside in my budget to give before spending for anything else. Giving to God's work must come first.

What is the Relationship Between Giving and Receiving?

➢ 2 Corinthians 9:6 "…He which _____ sparingly shall _____ also sparingly; and he which soweth _____ shall _____ also bountifully."

➢ Acts 20:35 "I have shewed you all things, how that so laboring ye ought to _____ the weak, and to remember the words of the Lord Jesus, how He said, 'It is more blessed to _____ than to receive.'"

➢ Malachi 3:8, 10, 11 "Will a man _____ God? Yet ye have robbed me. But ye say, 'Wherein have we _____ Thee?' In tithes and offerings…

v10 Bring ye all the _____ into the storehouse… and _____ Me now herewith, saith the Lord of Hosts, if I will not _____ you the _____ of _____, and pour you out a _____, that there shall not be room enough to _____ it,

v11 And I will rebuke the _____ for your sakes, and he shall not destroy the _____ of your ground; neither shall your _____ cast her fruit before the time in the field, saith the _____ of hosts."

➢ Luke 6:38 "_____, and it shall be given unto you; _____ down, and _____ together, and _____ over shall _____ give into your bosom. For with the same _____ that ye mete withal it shall be _____ to you again."

19. Tithing and Stewardship

Does God Want Me to Prosper?

➢ Psalms 35:27 "Let them shout for __ __ __ and be __ __ __ __, that favor my righteous cause: yea, let them say continually, let the Lord be magnified, which hath __ __ __ __ __ __ __ __ in the prosperity of His servant."

➢ Deuteronomy 8:18 "But thou shalt remember the Lord thy God: for it is He that giveth thee __ __ __ __ __ to get __ __ __ __ __ __, that He may establish His covenant which He sware unto thy fathers, as it is this day."

God promises to give us all we need to accomplish His will in our lives. He gives us as much more as we can handle without being spoiled (ruined). My giving to support the House of God is a sign of my being able to handle more wisely. So, if I give my tithe, God will bless me abundantly. Those blessings may be in the form of money or they may be in more important areas.

Money in itself is not evil. It is the LOVE of money and what it is spent for that brings trouble.

➢ 1 Timothy 6:10 "For the __ __ __ __ of money is the __ __ __ __ of all __ __ __ __ which while some __ __ __ __ __ __ __ after, they have __ __ __ __ __ from the faith, and pierced themselves through with many __ __ __ __ __ __ __."

Thoughts on giving
The Tithe
Abraham commenced it.
Jacob continued it.
Moses confirmed it.
Malachi commanded it
Christ commends it.

Give as you would if an angel awaited you at the church door.
Give as you would if tomorrow found your life were o're.
Give as you would to the Master if you met His loving look.
Give as you would of your substance if His hand your offering took.

Giving is a good thermometer of our spiritual warmth. Giving involves time, talent, treasure (money or possessions), love, and most important- ourselves.

20. Our church

You Need the Bread of Life

Jesus is the Bread of Life, the very source of Eternal life; just as physical bread is the "staff of [physical] life." We need the Bread of Life to live in our hearts, to help us with our everyday lives, and to guide us to Heaven. This is the ONLY way to get Eternal Life.

Christian Fellowship

God did not design us to be loners. He designed us to need each other, to need Christian Fellowship. That is what church is for; helping each other in our walk with God.

Church is supposed to be a place where you feel "at home," a place where, as the song says, "you can see, our troubles are all the same...where everybody knows your name, and their always glad you came. ...."

You and your family need to be a part of a bigger family.

You need us. And we need you.

Our History

Bread of Life Christian Fellowship held her first service May 1, 2001 in the Tracy home in Dayton. We also held Bible studies in Dave and Nancy Morton's home in south Carson City on Tuesday nights.

The property at 10042 hwy 50 East in Moundhouse was bought March 14 2002. It was completed and the final for holding service there was received on October 26, 2003. This property is owned by the church itself.

Our Government

Bread of Life has a Board of Elders made up of the Board of Deacons (the ministers of the church), and the Board of Trusties.
The Deacons are responsible for the Spiritual matters of the Church and the Trustee Board is responsible for the material matters.

We have a Meeting of the Membership once a year, usually the last

Wednesday of February. However, any time anyone has any question, we are happy to answer them.

Membership
In order to be a Voting Member of Bread of Life, you must attend regularly for six months; support the church financially, emotionally, and with your time. You must also have completed this study with a current member in good standing.

The Store
Bread of Life became a distributer for No Greater Joy ministry in 2004. We are able to buy resources from them at a discount so we can sell them affordably. All profits from NGJ materials go directly into buying more materials.

Several members of our congregation have written books. These have either been donated directly to the Church or are on consignment. Again, all the money the church gets goes back into purchasing more resources.

We do have a few other items for sale from other publishers, but we usually sell them at cost.

Missionaries
We support the Northern India Christian Ministries, an organization in the unreached areas of north India that trains local converts to be ministers in their own communities. They also have a school, college, and widow's training program. We try to have them visit us once a year.

Food Pantry
Each family in the church is asked to bring one can of food per week to add to our food pantry. (Some families just buy a couple of cases of food once a year at Smith's case sale). This food is used to help those we hear of who are in need.

    Our church website is http://www.BreadOfLifeCF.com
    Our email is OurChurch@BreadOfLifeCF.com
    Our phone number is 775-246-9997

20. Bread of Life Christian Fellowship

Our mailing address is:
>Bread of Life Christian Fellowship
>P.O. Box 20009
>Carson City, Nevada, 89721

God Bless.